LISA RENEE JONES

END GAME

HEADLINE
ETERNAL

The right of Lisa Renee Jones to be identified as the Author of
the Work has been asserted by her in accordance with the
Copyright, Designs and Patents Act 1988.

Published by arrangement with St Martin's Press

First published in Great Britain in 2018
by HEADLINE ETERNAL
An imprint of HEADLINE PUBLISHING GROUP

1

Cataloguing in Publication Data is available from the British Library

ISBN 978 1 4722 3813 9

Typeset in 11.16/14.72 pt Walbaum MT Std by Jouve (UK), Milton Keynes

Printed and bound in Great Britain by CPI Group (UK) Ltd, Croydon, CR0 4YY

MIX
Paper from
responsible sources
FSC® C104740

Headline's policy is to use papers that are natural, renewable and recyclable
products and made from wood grown in well-managed forests and other
controlled sources. The logging and manufacturing processes are expected
to conform to the environmental regulations of the country of origin.

HEADLINE PUBLISHING GROUP
An Hachette UK Company
Carmelite House
50 Victoria Embankment
London EC4Y 0DZ

www.headlineeternal.com
www.headline.co.uk
www.hachette.co.uk

To my readers:

Thank you for taking this journey with me and loving Shane and Emily's story as much as I could have ever hoped!

Xoxo,

Lisa

Dear Readers,

It's that time again. The time I hate and dread but also enjoy so much. You finally get to read the finale to Shane and Emily's story . . . for now. I never like to say goodbye to my characters, but I am leaving you with my current version of their happily ever after. That's not a spoiler! It is a romance, after all. But how they'll get there . . . you'll just have to read to find out! This book packed a much bigger emotional punch than I ever anticipated. Just ask my husband—he walked in on me several times blubbering over these characters who have become so beloved and important to me. I know *Bad Deeds* left off on a heart-wrenching cliffhanger. And for that, I'm still sorry! But it had to happen. As much as I wield the keystrokes, these characters dictate their own stories.

BEFORE YOU GO ANY FURTHER! Please be sure you've read *Hard Rules, Damage Control,* and *Bad Deeds* (in that order) before reading on. I'm about to recap *Bad Deeds* since a bit of time has passed for some readers who read it when it first came out, and the following paragraphs will have spoilers for the previous books and prepare you for how *End Game* will begin.

As a refresher: we picked up in *Bad Deeds* after Derek's threat to Emily at the family dinner with him, Shane, Brandon Senior, and Maggie. This is also following Adrian having stabbed Derek in the hand when he learned about his payoff to the FBI agent, and that the FBI was now snooping around Brandon Pharmaceuticals, which Adrian has infiltrated with his drug trade.

After Derek's not-so-veiled threat, Emily is visibly shaken, but eventually she shores up her tough attitude to go back in for dinner. Brandon Senior has announced a new trial that could result in remission for his cancer. That comes as a shock to everyone, and he announces that Maggie will be joining him for a two-week stint in Germany for the treatment. In his absence, Shane will be taking over Brandon Enterprises, much to Derek's outrage.

Following these major shifts in this dangerous game, Emily and Shane return to their apartment, where they find Adrian Martina waiting for them, unannounced and uninvited. He has a business proposition for Shane: help bring the Martina cartel even further into Brandon Pharmaceuticals' operations by allowing the consortium he is part of to invest, and get their illegal drug past FDA testing and on the legal market. Of course, Shane is against the proposal, but if he wants to get everyone out of this fight alive, he has to play his cards smart. Which does not sit well with Emily. She wants herself and Shane as far away from the drug cartel as possible. After Adrian's goodbye, and a tense debate with Emily about the Martina cartel, Shane leaves to game-plan with Seth and Nick. They've decided Emily will need a protective detail after the events of Adrian stabbing Derek and as tensions get higher as they are about to make their move to extricate the cartel from BP. They also find out that Ted, one of Nick's men, is missing and has been since Adrian paid Shane a visit. Of course, they soon realize this is a scare tactic for Shane and his family by Martina, which comes to a head when Ted is delivered in a box during what seems to be an attack on the office building. Making for a very public display and a skittish and more alert group.

Shane is also still reeling from the information that his mother has been having an affair with Mike Rogers, one of the stockholders in BE and the owner of a national basketball team. He also finds that Mike is trying to conduct a hostile takeover of BE, which just adds insult to injury. Shane can't let Mike or Adrian take his family's legacy from him. As their parents jet off to Germany, Derek and Shane visit Mike Rogers, only to be slapped with an impending lawsuit for control of the company now that their father is gone and seemingly unfit to run it. So Derek and Shane, unlikely cohorts, team up in the face of their adversaries, and create the plan to sell off Brandon Pharmaceuticals (the most profitable branch) from Brandon Enterprises to Mike Rogers, whom Adrian will be able to control with no problem, and buy up Mike's team's sports center for Adrian's consortium investors so Adrian has even more leverage over Mike. This will extricate both Mike and Adrian from Brandon Enterprises entirely.

Who we see much more of in *Bad Deeds* is Teresa Martina, Adrian's sister and Derek's lover. She's very at odds with what the right thing to do is: she loves Derek, but she doesn't want to be the cause of his loss of life because of who her brother is either. She also has an infatuated member of Adrian's team, Ramon, who is obsessed with her and sketchily following Emily as well. Teresa eventually leaves Derek for his own good, which devastates him.

All this takes place while Emily and Shane have been planning to create an incorruptible branch of Brandon Enterprises—a fashion and makeup line—which will more than make up their profit losses from the sell-offs to Mike. Before any of this can be implemented, though, with Derek drunk and distraught over Teresa, and Emily being caught unaware, they are both kidnapped by Ramon. Ramon has heard Adrian talking about legalizing the cartel business, which he blames Shane and Adrian for; this does not fit his motives at all, and complicates his obsession over Teresa and her love for Derek. He's incredibly unstable, and when Shane shows up to save Derek and Emily, Ramon and Shane both fire off shots, with Shane killing Ramon. Ramon's gun is pointed at Emily, but

Derek jumps in front of it to try to save her. And those are the last heart-stopping moments of *Bad Deeds*. Shane's agonizing cry as he sees his brother, who is finally coming back to him, and the woman he loves immeasurably, both falling to the floor, both covered in blood . . . which is right where we pick up in *End Game*. . . .

Xoxo,
Lisa

CAST OF CHARACTERS

EMILY STEVENS (27)—Heroine in the series. film is Brandon Senior's newly appointed secretary. After landing her new job, she learns that the one-night stand she had the night before turns out to be her boss's son Shane Brandon. Emily has secrets and she's running. But Shane will not let her run from him. During *Hard Rules*, the two had a lot of push and pull about their relationship, his family, and her secrets.

SHANE BRANDON (32)—Hero of the series. Shane Brandon is the black sheep of the family. The good one. The one willing to risk everything to play this game on the up-and-up and keep his brother from ruining the family empire, Brandon Enterprises, by getting in bed with the Martina family drug cartel. But Shane is treading on thin ice as he bring his legacy back from the brink of corruption. He is also dealing with Emily Stevens. A woman who breaks through his defenses and brings an innocence to his life that he can't have as a distraction. He wants and needs to protect her, possess her, and be worthy of her. She is already making him a better man and keeping him grounded. But she has secrets, and could be the one to ultimately send his world crumbling harder than he ever anticipated.

DEREK BRANDON (37)—The older brother. While he's brilliant and good-looking, his greed for power drives him to make rash decisions. He and Shane were close as kids, but once they became adults and Shane joined Brandon Enterprises, that shifted. Everything became about who would control the empire. Derek has gotten the family corporation into bed with the Martina drug cartel, and Shane will do everything in his power to stop his brother.

MAGGIE BRANDON—Shane and Derek's mother. Seemingly befriending Emily, yet we are uncertain about her ultimate motives concerning the current struggle between her sons for control over Brandon Enterprises. Married to David Brandon (Brandon Senior).

DAVID BRANDON—The head of Brandon Enterprises and the Brandon family. Father to Derek and Shane. Husband to Maggie. He is dying of cancer but wants to leave a legacy and hold on to control of Brandon Enterprises as long as possible. He's a bastard and pushes Shane and Derek in all the wrong ways. He is gruff, cold, and hard at every turn. He enjoys watching his sons battle for power. It entertains him.

SETH CAGE (35)—Shane's right-hand man. Ex-CIA. Shane recruited Seth from their firm in New York, and Seth has now become the head of security at Brandon Enterprises.

JESSICA (29)—Shane's assistant. Ever the loyal employee, she followed him from New York and becomes friends with Emily as Emily starts to work as Brandon Senior's assistant. Jessica's job knows no bounds, as she helps Shane with everything from securing a new apartment to keeping an eye on Brandon Senior and Derek and relaying any curious goings-on when Shane is not in the office.

ERIC KNIGHT—A friend of Shane's from college who is a brilliant surgeon and has squeaky-clean morals. Eric is the doctor of the patient who was running her mouth about Brandon Pharmaceuticals (BP, and part of Brandon Enterprises) being the distributor for an undetectable performance-enhancing drug that her Major League Baseball player husband is taking. Eric brings this news to Shane, causing Shane to take action.

ADRIAN MARTINA—The son of the Mexican cartel leader, Roberto Martinez. Runs the US side of the cartel's operations. He has some relationship with Derek Brandon, the extent of which is not fully known yet. Brother to Teresa Martina, who is sleeping with Derek.

TERESA MARTINA—Sister to Adrian. Sleeping with Derek. Bartender at Martina's Casa.

RANDY—Security guard of the building where the Brandon Enterprises offices are located. Emily and Shane have a conversation with him over her missing cell phone. Keeps Shane updated on his father's activities.

MIKE ROGERS—Sits on the board of Brandon Enterprises. Holds 20 percent of its stock and owns a professional basketball team. Key player in the hedge fund as well. Has a lot to lose if Brandon Enterprises were to shut down its investment division. His company, Rogers Athletics, is one of the proposed investments for the hedge fund. When Seth and Shane are trying to dig up dirt on the board members so they will swing their way in a vote for power of the company, Seth cannot find anything substantial on Mike.

RICK STEVENS—Emily's brother. Is aware of her secrets and why she is hiding. He's very hard for Emily to get in touch with, and his silence and evasiveness make Emily nervous.

LANA SMITH—A brilliant scientist and businessperson at Brandon Pharmaceuticals. She wants Shane and has caused him trouble in the past. She hid weed in his car and almost cost him his attendance at Harvard. She caused a slight rift between him and Emily in *Hard Rules* and is still trying to get close to him now.

NICK SNYDER—Knows Seth from their CIA/FBI days. Saved Seth's life, and now Seth has brought him to Shane so Nick can help get to the bottom of the true involvement of the Martina cartel in Brandon Enterprises. Confirms that the Brandon Enterprises trucking division is already distributing cocaine. Is going to help Shane and Seth figure out how to maneuver a takedown and extricate the company out of the hold of the Martina cartel.

CODY RODRIGUEZ—Part of Nick's team. Appointed as Emily's bodyguard/detail. In *Bad Deeds* he and Jessica were given food poisoning in order to distract them while Emily was kidnapped and held hostage along with Derek.

CAST OF CHARACTERS

ROY GIVENS—Potential investor in the sports center. Someone who Shane will have to contend with.

FREDDY "MAVERICK" WOODS—Shane's old boss and the lead partner at his old firm. Has been trying desperately to bring Shane back into the firm since he left for Denver.

END
GAME

PART ONE

THE GRIM REAPER

SHANE

CHAPTER ONE

"I will live to hurt you. I will live to torture you. You will die a slow, painful death for this."

Adrian Martina, drug lord and monster that he is, doesn't react to my guttural vow, nor does he react to my brother and the woman I love lying on the floor next to me, blood all over them and me. But I react. I jolt out of my shock at finding them like this, and shout up at him, "Get me a damn ambulance!" even as my fingers search Derek's and Emily's necks for pulses. The momentary joy I find in discovering Emily has one is doused by how pale and still she is, and how weak, nearly non-existent, the heartbeat I finally find in Derek proves to be.

It's then that a shiver of foreboding rips through me, and my gaze rockets to Adrian just in time to find him pulling a gun. But I don't have time to call him the chicken-shit bastard he clearly is before he's lifted the barrel over my head and fired, the sound jolting me. One time. Two. Ironically, considering Martina's very existence is why we are here now, I feel relief and find clarity of mind by the third shot. Martina needs me for financial gain, and I turn my attention back to those who need me and actually matter: Derek and Emily. The stickiness under my hand where it rests on Derek's chest tells me he's in real trouble. From that moment everything goes in slow motion, like I'm in a tunnel, despite how fast I feel like I'm moving. I confirm that Emily isn't bleeding, but she still isn't moving, while Derek's pulse remains faint and he has two bullet holes in his chest, draining like faucets.

"Fuck," I breathe out, adrenaline jolting me, my hands pressing to the wounds. "Get me a damn ambulance!" I shout again, climbing over Derek to keep Emily in my view, my gaze swinging left to find Ramon lying at Derek's feet. "Get me a goddamn ambulance now!"

Adrian's voice carries as a loud shout in the air before he is kneeling on the opposite side of Derek. "Help's on the way," he announces, adding, "and this was Ramon's doing, not mine."

Ignoring his claim of innocence, I eye his neck and then him. "Take off your tie," I order, my blood-soaked jeans and T-shirt of little to no use to prepare the tourniquet Derek needs. I hope. I really have no fucking clue what I'm doing right now.

"You keep the pressure on the wounds," he says, removing the tie. "I'll pull this underneath him."

"Do it," I say, with no misconception about his willingness to help. This is about his concern that Derek's and Emily's safety, or rather lack thereof, might impact my willingness to get him the money I vowed to give him to get him the hell out of my company. The problem for him is that it's too late for a business deal to end our relationship with any ray of light. I'm going to kill him and succeed in doing so where others have failed, but first: we save the ones I love.

He shouts out to his men, and in a matter of seconds, it

seems, we have towels, which he's tearing and knotting together. We wrap those around Derek's chest, and the process is bloody and brutal to me, but to Derek, there is nothing. He doesn't move. He doesn't react. Not to the towels or the tie and belts we use to cut the blood flow. We've just finished doing about everything I believe we can do when I hear, "Shane. What the hell is going—Holy hell."

At the sound of Eric's voice, my gaze jerks to the doorway to find him standing just inside the room, one of Adrian's goons on either side of him, each holding an arm. Eric is dressed in pajamas, no doubt already in bed to prep for his early morning surgeries, when he was grabbed and brought here. "This is your version of help?" I demand, my gaze swinging to Adrian's, my lips thinning. "He doesn't belong in this."

"He can help," Adrian says. "And we need help."

"Help is called 'an ambulance,'" I bite out. "The one you didn't call, did you?"

"Let go of me," Eric demands, jerking away from the two men holding him to quickly rush to Emily's side, kneeling beside her to check her pulse and scalp. "Stable, but with a head injury," he announces, already moving toward me. "What do we have?" he asks, motioning to have me inch toward Derek's legs to allow him to position himself next to my brother's chest.

"Two obvious bullet wounds," I say, watching as Eric presses his fingers to Derek's neck. "There was a lot of blood," I add. "I can't be sure there wasn't another entry point."

"No point of exit for the bullets," Adrian adds. "He needs surgery. Good thing you're a surgeon."

Eric's gaze rockets to Adrian. "He won't survive it without blood. And even if he could, I'm not that kind of surgeon. I'll kill him."

"Buy him some time," Adrian orders.

"He needs blood and an ambulance," Eric insists. "Lots of blood that I don't carry around in my pocket. An ambulance should have beaten me here."

"Did you or did you not call an ambulance?" I demand.

"It'll be here," Adrian assures me. "And when it arrives, we need our facts straight. Stick to the truth. Ramon was jealous of Derek and Teresa. You had words with him over Derek, and we all assume he targeted Emily to pay you back." He snaps his fingers and a man steps forward. "Martin here killed him to save us."

"You killed him," I say.

"I killed him," the other man assures me.

Sirens sound in the not-so-distant distance. "Your ambulance," Adrian says. "As promised."

I narrow my stare at him. "If you knew that ambulance was coming, why is Eric here? Why suggest he do surgery?"

"I believe in taking precautions," he says, and before I can repeat Eric's observation that the ambulance should have beat him here, Adrian adds, "and your brother's dire circumstances said he didn't have much time."

"No thanks to you," I say, pushing to my feet as he does the same, and I can feel the façade of control I'm clinging to begin to crack. "And we both know," I add, the two of us glaring at each other over my brother's body, "that 'buy him some time' means you were covering something up before you called for help."

"The ambulance was called," he repeats, his tone as sharp as the knife of emotion cutting through me.

"Not soon enough," I say, and snap, lunging toward him only to have Eric suddenly grab my shoulders.

"Derek," he says. "Think of Derek."

"I am thinking of Derek," I grind out. "And Emily."

"Later," he says. "Do this later."

Voices sound in the building, and suddenly the paramedics are rushing into the room, dissolving the tension in the air and replacing it with urgency and chaos. I back up, giving the uniformed men space as Adrian does the same. Eric, on the other hand, stands in the mix of things, helping the crew. I'm pushed back farther, and Adrian and I end up standing side by side, watching them work. But he's not present to me. There is just me, alone, waiting to hear if the woman I want to be my wife and the brother I love no matter what his flaws live or die.

I can see the paramedics working feverishly to insert IVs into both Derek and Emily, one of them calling ahead for blood as they do. I'm outside the restaurant as Derek and Emily are rolled toward two separate ambulances.

"You can only go with one of them," Eric says. "I'll go with Derek in case he needs help. You go with Emily."

With that offer, he's saved me the torment of deciding between the two, and I nod my appreciation, quickly moving to Emily's side, where a paramedic is adjusting her IV, looking less than pleased for some reason. "I'm her husband," I say with zero hesitation. "Is there a problem beyond the obvious head injury?"

"Just trying to get the fluid moving properly," he says, his attention on her arm, not me, and I reach for her delicate little hand. It's cold. Her face is pale. My heart is breaking. I lean in close to her cheek, my mouth near her ear. "I need you, woman. You can't leave me. That's an order."

"We need to get her into the vehicle," the paramedic says while another appears beside me and forces me to once again back away from someone I love, and trust her to someone else. It's killing me. Driving me out of my fucking mind.

"Shane."

I rotate to find Eric standing outside the ambulance. "He's asking for you. Come. I'll go with Emily." I see Emily's stretcher being lifted into the ambulance, and by the time I turn to Eric again, he's in front of me.

"He's not good, man," he warns, his hand on my shoulder, when he might as well have dug a blade into my chest. "Be with him," he encourages. "I'll take care of Emily." He eyes the paramedic and me. "Go now before they leave us both." He takes off to the ambulance with Emily inside, and I watch as the doors to Derek's ambulance begin to close.

"Wait!" I call out, charging forward. "I'm his brother. I'm coming with you."

"Shane?" the man asks.

"Yes. Shane."

He gives a nod and inches the door open, backing up to allow my entry. I climb inside, and I don't have to ask how the paramedic knew my name. Derek moans out, "Shane," from his stretcher, his eyes shut, a monitor to the right of him, while the paramedic maneuvers to allow me to take a spot to the left of Derek.

"I'm here," I say, kneeling beside him, the doors shutting with a thundering crash as I do, sirens screeching through the air, with the promise that death is on the run. "I'm here." I repeat.

His lashes flutter and his eyes open. "Shane," he whispers, but even as he looks at me, I'm not sure he really sees me.

"Yes," I say. "Shane. It's me. I'm here." I pull his hand into mine. And it's cold. Too damn cold. *"I'm here,"* I repeat, because as much as I want to tell him that he's going to be okay, and as fucked up as our family is, I myself have never lied to him. I'm not going to start now. Maybe I should. Maybe a bittersweet lie is what he needs to hear.

"Emily?" he asks.

"She's stable."

"What . . . what . . ."

"She hit her head."

"Damn it," he curses, blood pooling on his lip. "I tried . . ."

"You saved her," I assure him, his words and his distress telling me I was right. He took those bullets for her. "She hit her head. She'll be okay." Words I refuse to accept as one of the lies I swore I wouldn't tell.

"I didn't mean . . . Things just . . ."

"I know," I say, glancing at his monitor and noting his low blood pressure with concern. "We'll get through this," I add, refocusing on him.

"Fuck Martina," he whispers, his expression fierce. "Save . . . our company."

"We'll save it together when you get well."

"Promise me. Promise . . . you will . . . save—"

I squeeze his hand. "Derek."

"Promise me, damn it."

"I promise," I say, hating the sense of "the end" he's giving me.

His lashes lower and lift. "Teresa . . . tell Teresa . . . I . . . love her."

"You can tell her."

"Tell her, Shane." There's a white line around his lips that seems to thicken. "Please."

"I will," I promise. "I'll tell her."

"One . . . last thing . . ."

"Okay," I say, that word "last" grinding through me. "What is it?"

"Tell Pops . . . tell him . . . I'll see him in hell, and he . . . won't be king." His lashes lower again and his expression

relaxes, as if he's at peace with our exchange. Or just unconscious. "Is his blood pressure a problem?" I ask, turning to the
paramedic.

"Yes," the man says. "But we can't do much more until we
get to the hospital."

"How long?"

"Another five minutes."

Another five minutes, in which I will have no idea what
Emily's condition is, while praying I don't watch my brother
die, will be hell. I've no sooner finished that thought when
Derek's monitor flatlines.

CHAPTER TWO

The next few minutes prove there really is a hell on earth.

I watch as the paramedic works on Derek, and somehow, by the time we pull into the hospital driveway, Derek's heart is beating again. He's breathing, but I'm not sure I am. Even before the vehicle pauses, the doors of the ambulance are yanked open and I just get the hell out of the way, exiting and allowing the paramedics to lift Derek's stretcher, and him with it, out of the vehicle. A cluster of people instantly surround him, instructions being shouted, the bed being rolled toward the hospital entrance.

Double-stepping to keep pace, I scan for Emily's ambulance, an iron fist around my heart at her absence. "Where the fuck is she?" I murmur, pulling my phone from my pocket as Seth appears out of nowhere.

"What the hell happened in that restaurant?" he asks, making this the first time I've seen him since Ramon's men blocked his entry into Martina's place with me.

"Aside from finding them both in their present conditions,"

I say, "my brother took a couple of bullets for Emily." I punch Eric's number into my cell as he exits the sliding glass doors in front of us, blood streaking his clothes. "Where's Emily?" I demand, returning my phone to my blood-drenched pocket.

"They took her back for tests," he says, "but they need a responsible party to sign her in."

I nod and step around him, entering the emergency room and heading to the counter to greet the female attendant in scrubs behind it. "My brother and my wife were just admitted," I say with no hesitation in claiming that bond with Emily for personal and legal reasons. She might not be my wife yet, but she will be soon if I have my way. If she'll still have me at all. If I should even dare believe I can be worthy of her now.

The attendant eyes my bloodstained shirt, her expression unchanged as she says, "I'll need insurance or credit card information."

I remove my wallet and slide the company insurance information across the counter, along with my black Amex card. Questions and paperwork follow, and I arrange for the private wing, the place the elite go to hide from the press. Because right now any press linking our family to a cartel is the last thing we need. I've finally finished what needs to be finished when I hear, "Mr. Brandon."

Turning, I find a police officer standing with Seth and Eric. "Yes?" I ask, irritated at the timing, impatient for an update on Derek and Emily.

"Can we ask you some questions?"

"You can ask me to read you the dictionary for all I care," I say. "But not until I know my brother and my wife are stable." Neither Seth nor Eric blink at my reference to Emily as my wife, and I don't wait for the officer to agree or disagree with anything I have to say. I offer him my back and return my attention to the desk. "I need to know what's happening to them now."

"The Brandon family! I need the Brandon family."

At the shout from the other side of the room, I rotate and spot a woman in scrubs as the source of the inquiry. "Here!" I call out, ignoring the police officer still hovering, and making a beeline for her by way of the packed waiting area. "I'm Shane Brandon," I say, stopping in front of her. "Derek's my brother. How is he? And my wife. Emily. She was—"

"She's stable and unconscious," she says. "They're running a CT scan on her now and then we'll get her to a room."

"Stable," I repeat, not prepared to have that equal relief. "Are you the doctor?"

"A nurse," she corrects me.

"And you've been told she's stable?"

"Yes."

"Defined as what?"

"Defined as stable," she repeats. "And in testing right now. Your brother, however, is in critical condition. Aside from losing a dangerous amount of blood, one of the bullets is lodged in his heart."

My own heart damn nearly stops beating. "And?"

"He's in surgery. If you'd like to come with me, we can get you set up in the private waiting area until your wife and brother are situated in rooms."

"I've talked to the front desk about setting Derek and Emily up in the private wing," I say. "I assume that's in progress."

"If you've set it up, it'll happen," she says, and without waiting for my reply, she turns away, pushing through a set of double doors. I follow, the scent of sickness and death scorching my nostrils, while Seth and Eric appear on either side of me, the police officer thankfully gone now. Eric should be as well, and I'd tell him as much, but the nurse stops in front of a doorway and faces me, or rather us, her gaze shifting between Eric and Seth then back to me. "I'll have one of the aides bring a few pairs of scrubs."

I give a curt nod, but she's already rushing away. Peering into the small, boxy waiting area, I confirm it's empty and enter the room, seeing fifteen or so chairs—some down the middle and others lining the walls to the left and right of me. A large window is the only thing distinguishing it from an oversized casket about to suck me in and do me in all at once.

"You need to leave before you get any deeper into this," I say, rotating to face Seth and Eric, my attention on Eric.

Eric gives a bitter laugh and lifts his hands at his sides. "I'm covered in blood. I'm as deep as it gets. And we both know I wasn't brought there tonight to simply walk away. What the hell was that back there?"

I eye Seth with a silent question he answers without hesitation. "Martina just enlisted you as his newly anointed cartel doctor, is my assumption."

"Holy hell," Eric growls, scrubbing his jaw, which manages to be clean-shaven despite the late hour. "No," he adds. "No, that isn't happening. I saw nothing to give him that kind of control over me. And I agreed to absolutely nothing."

"This wasn't about your agreement," Seth says. "This was a test. He measured your reactions under pressure. Unless you failed, and I doubt you did, he'll create whatever ammunition is needed to ensure you respond when he needs you to respond."

"No," I say, meeting Eric's stare. "That's not going to happen. That's not what he meant to happen."

"Then what did he mean to happen, Shane?" Eric demands.

My jaw sets as the realization of just what a bastard Martina really is hits me. "He needs leverage to control me after tonight. I'll handle it. Go home."

"Leverage, why?" he questions. "What are you involved in?"

"Derek got into bed with Martina's sister and showed up on Ramon's radar for that reason," I say, telling him nothing more. "Just as you were told."

"And Martina's part of a drug cartel," Eric supplies.

"Yes," I say, again telling him as little as possible.

"And he needs ammunition against you, why?" he presses.

Seth and I exchange a look, and Seth replies with, "It's who he is," Seth says. "It's what he does."

The non-answer earns Seth a look of irritation from Eric. "He wants me to negotiate your freedom," I say.

"Negotiate," he repeats. "So I'm ammunition against you."

"Correct."

"What does he want from you, Shane?"

"This doesn't concern you, Eric," I state.

"After tonight, it concerns me," he snaps. "I have a right to ask questions."

"You have a right to get the hell out of this," I say.

"Distance yourself," Seth urges. "Far away. In fact, take a vacation for a couple of weeks."

"I have surgeries scheduled," he states. "I'm not taking a vacation."

"Knock, knock," a female voice says, and we all look toward the door to find a woman in some sort of flowery scrub shirt, indicating the green scrubs in her hands. "I brought clothes."

Seth moves toward her and takes them while I get to what's important. "Any news for us otherwise?"

"Sorry," she says. "I'm just an aide. I don't have any news at all." She disappears into the hallway while Seth hands a set of scrubs to Eric.

"Change. Then go home, Eric."

Eric ignores him and focuses on me. "Shane——"

"Go the *fuck* home," I order. "You're safe."

"Seth just told me to leave town," he reminds me. "That doesn't feel safe."

"Because you can't stop asking questions," Seth states irritably. "And you need to. Which is exactly why I'll have a man escort you to your house and we'll watch it until this passes. Not to keep you safe. To keep you out of this."

Again, Eric ignores Seth and speaks to me. "How, exactly, is it going to pass?"

"My way," I assure him.

His lips thin. "I'm not leaving until I know Derek and Emily are stable."

"The longer you stay," I say, "the more power you give Martina to pull you into this." I inhale a heavy breath and let it out. "Look. I appreciate the hell out of what you did tonight. I owe you in ways I can't ever repay. But I need you to leave. Now."

"What does he want from you, Shane?" Eric presses.

"If he's smart," I say, "to keep breathing." My jaw sets. "Eric——"

"I'll go," he bites out. "But I need an update on Derek and Emily as soon as you get one."

"I'll make sure of it," Seth promises.

Eric finally offers us an agreeable nod and accepts the scrubs Seth is still trying to shove his way, before turning and heading for the door. I inhale again, this breath a bit thinner, easier. Once he's gone, I face the window without seeing anything beyond the glass. There is just Emily's pale face and Derek's bloodied body. "You should change," Seth suggests. "The blood just reminds the police they need to talk to you."

"I should have gone to dinner with her," I say, cutting him a look, my mind going to Jessica's panicked phone call and the details she shared. "Cody," I say. "Jessica said they were poisoned right before Emily was kidnapped."

"He was admitted for the night here, at this hospital, about two hours ago," he says. "Jessica wasn't anywhere near in his condition."

"She wasn't admitted?"

"No, but they pumped Cody's stomach and filled him with counteractive drugs of some sort. And still he manages to ask about Emily. He feels like he let her and you down."

"I let her down," I say, my throat raw with the admission I won't hide from. "I should have gotten her the hell out of this city until Martina was out of the picture."

"Obviously, you need to be reminded as to why that wasn't possible. Martina would have seen that as a war cry. He would have followed her. He would—"

"I get it," I snap, cutting him a sharp look. "I know the reasons and they weren't good enough."

His expression tightens and he faces the window while I do the same. "What about your parents?" he finally asks. "When are you going to call them?"

"My father's in Germany, fighting for his life," I say. "My mother's there, watching it happen, and no matter what their relationship, that has to be hell. Nothing good can come out of me calling either of them now."

There's a shift in the air, and Seth and I rotate to find a thirtysomething man in a gray suit, a good two-day stubble on his jaw, standing in the doorway. "Mr. Brandon and Mr. Cage."

"And you are?" Seth asks, his tone sharp, his energy sharper.

The man reaches into his pocket and removes a badge. "Federal Agent Brian Dennis."

This news sits about as easily as gasoline, considering I've spent months avoiding FBI involvement with Brandon Enterprises and that Martina himself has now shoved them right up my fucking ass. "What can we do for you, Agent?" I ask, my tone even, unaffected, while that precious control I value is teetering on the edge of expulsion.

He gives my bloodstained clothes a once-over before narrowing his eyes at me. "It's more what I can do for you."

"Unless you came to tell me my brother and wife are both fully recovered, there isn't much you can do for me right now," I assure him.

He glances at Seth. "We need a minute."

Seth looks at me, and I motion for his departure, and while his expression remains unchanged, I sense the crackle of unease in him, the hesitation, before he heads to the hallway. The agent claims a chair by the wall, no doubt trying to pull down my defenses by leaving me in a power position. It's reverse psychology, and I don't like being toyed with. I don't like other people being in control, which is exactly what I've allowed to happen, or my woman and my brother wouldn't be fighting for their lives right now. Removing the agent's perceived upper hand, I sit in one of the chairs lined up down the middle of the room, directly across from him.

"All right, Agent Dennis," I say. "You obviously want to talk, so talk. But be clear. The minute they walk in here with news about my brother or my woman, this conversation ends. Make your minutes count."

He takes me at my word and gets right to the point. "Why are you involved with Martina?"

"I'll be as direct as you just were," I reply. "The short version. My brother met Martina's sister, Teresa, and fell in love. Ramon was in love with Teresa, and the rest is pretty obvious."

"That explains your brother's involvement with Martina, but not yours."

"I wanted my brother out of the Martina circle," I say. "That didn't go over well with my brother, who insisted Martina was legit and that I was an asshole for judging him by his father, considering our father is no one either of us wants to claim as our role model." And because I am now certain they've been watching, I add, "I met Adrian. He showed up to welcome me to the family. I saw who he was that day. I knew I was right about him, and thus I worked to get my brother the hell away from him and Teresa."

"Obviously, you failed."

"Ironically, the bitter pill to this is that I did not. Teresa wanted to protect him as well. She left him and it jolted him enough to get him to step away from the company. He was leaving the city."

He stares at me several long beats, calculation in his brown eyes. "Help me get him."

"Ramon's dead."

"We both know I'm not talking about Ramon."

Anger comes at me hard and fast. "Let me get this straight," I say, leaning forward, my elbows on my knees. "My brother and my woman could be dead before this night is out, and you see this as an opportunity to recruit me to help you." I stand up. "Conversation over."

He pushes to his feet. "Your association with Martina is a dangerous one."

"Whatever threat you think to issue is not only poorly

timed, but misplaced. And whoever else you might intimidate with your badge, I'm not on the list."

"We both know Brandon Enterprises has gray areas, something you shared a little too legitimately with Martina."

"If you're on a witch hunt," I say, "you're going to need an attorney as good as me to fight me, and you won't find one."

His jaw sets hard and he scrubs it, that stubble of his giving a loud rasp. "Look." He presses his hands to his hips. "My timing isn't the best here, but I won't apologize for wanting to take down Martina. He's a monster hiding in a two-thousand-dollar suit."

"He wouldn't be seen in a two-thousand-dollar suit. It would be beneath him at that price tag, which tells me you don't know him. Figure him out or you'll never take him down."

"Help me."

"No," I say. "My family had a brush with that man, and you see where that got them."

Our eyes lock and hold. "I don't believe for a minute you're going to let him get away with this."

"Ramon did this. Not Martina."

"You don't believe that."

"No, Agent. That's my final answer."

"I'll ask again."

"You mean you'll look for a way to force my hand. I can promise you, you won't find it. I've taken over the company for a reason. We do things right. And right doesn't involve you."

He stares at me for several heavy beats before he says, "Good luck with your family," and heads toward the door, pausing to turn and face me again. "Wearing those bloodstained clothes is like wearing the self-blame and guilt. You might even decide it's what you deserve, but those things can be dangerous if unchecked. No telling where it might lead you, and me."

He turns and exits with the promise that he's watching me, his intent clear. He wants to box me into helping him, but I don't want his form of justice. I want revenge. Sweet, bloody revenge: on Martina, for playing the games he played with my brother and my company. On Mike Rogers for fucking my mother and trying to take over our company. And on my fucking father, who pitted us all against one another and gave Martina a weakness to invade. Only, cancer is already taking its revenge on my father.

Eyeing the change of clothes Seth's left on a chair for me, I snatch them up and exit into the hallway to find Seth talking with Agent Dennis. Ignoring them both, I enter the bathroom directly across from the lobby and lock the door. Alone now, out of anyone else's view, I allow myself the first real breath I've taken since finding Derek and Emily in that office. I lean against the door, squeezing my eyes shut, my temples throbbing, that moment when I had to leave Emily on the floor to attend to Derek slicing through me. Then again, when I had to leave her in an ambulance alone, to ride with Derek to the hospital. What if he lives and she dies, and I wasn't there for her?

What if they both die?

I shove off of the door, my hands balling into fists, the urge to hit something, or someone, almost too much to bear. Anger and pain consume me. I can't fix this. I'm helpless. I should have done so many things differently, and my gaze goes skyward. "Please, God. I know I don't talk to you often. I know I'm not the most religious man, but I try to be a good man. I try to do what is right. Please save them. Please heal them."

My hands come down on the sink, and I think of the blood spilled tonight and the blood I want in return. "Save them and I won't kill him," I vow, opening my eyes to look in the mirror, blood streaking my cheek, and while blood is not familiar to me, it is to Adrian Martina. If Derek or Emily dies, my loss will be nothing to him. "I have to kill him," I say, looking skyward again. "I can't tell you that I won't kill him. He needs to be sent to hell even if I have to go with him."

Resolved with that decision, I push off the sink and strip out of my jeans, jacket, and once-white T-shirt, replacing them with the clean scrubs before splashing water onto my face. Drying off, feeling a bit more human, I consider tossing my clothes into the trash, but the detective's words come back to me: *Wearing those bloodstained clothes is like wearing the self-blame and guilt. You might even decide it's what you deserve, but those things can be dangerous if unchecked.*

Dangerous.

Me.

Unchecked.

Yes, I am.

And everyone responsible for today is going to find that out.

I'm keeping the clothes and the memories they represent.

CHAPTER THREE

I've just embraced how dangerous my guilt can be when a knock sounds on the door, followed by Seth calling out, "Shane."

I yank the door open to find a woman in scrubs standing in front of me, Seth hovering behind her. "What is it?" I ask, bands of tension radiating up my spine as I wait for whatever this piece of news might be.

"Your wife's out of testing," she says, and just the inference that Emily's alive delivers a small piece of relief. "We've set her up in one of your private rooms. The doctor would like to speak to you."

"How is she?" I ask, stepping into the hallway and wanting some good news now, not later.

"I was told she's still stable," she says, "but I'm an aide. That's all I know." She gives an awkward gesture over her shoulder. "This way."

She starts walking, and Seth and I fall into step with her, each at one of her shoulders. "How's my brother?"

"He's still in surgery," she informs me.

"It's been at least an hour," I point out.

She directs us down a hallway to an elevator. "I really don't know anything but what I'm told. I'm sorry."

The elevator doors open and we step inside the car. Once there, the aide punches in the seventh floor, and the instant the ride begins, I flash back to the moment Derek flatlined in the ambulance; once again, I'm replaying the list of mistakes I've made, too long to even complete before we've finished the short ride. The doors part, and we follow the aide into a hallway, walking a long path that leads us to yet another hallway that leads to double doors. "This is your private suite," she informs us, keying in a code. "One-eight-one-eight," she says as the doors buzz open. "That will be your security code, which will remain intact until you depart."

I take in the information, but I'm focused on one thing: Emily, who is on the other side of these doors, but I manage an agreeable nod and follow the aide inside. She pauses just past the entrance to wait on me. "I'll leave you to the medical staff," she says, stepping around me while Seth holds the door for her, but I'm already moving forward, eager for news on Emily. Desperate to see her and touch her, I round the corner to enter what equates to a giant suite, with a living area and kitchen to the right. But most important, to my left, there is a hospital room setup that includes a bed, and the sight of Emily on top of it, tubes in her mouth and arms, punches me in the chest.

Beside her bed, a tall man wearing blue scrubs, who I estimate to be in his forties, is speaking to the nurse I met in the lobby. Both seem to sense my presence at the same moment, ending their conversation to turn to me. "Mr. Brandon," the man says, returning Emily's chart to the side of the bed. "I'm Dr. Milbourn."

"How is she?" I ask, walking toward her and him, only to have him do the same, placing himself between me and the bed, his tall, lanky body a wall between me and Emily that I want removed.

"She's—"

"Stable," I supply, anticipating what he's about to say. "I keep hearing that. What does that mean?"

"Her scan shows swelling of the brain."

"Swelling," I repeat. "Of the brain. That doesn't sound stable."

"As dramatic as this sounds, in reality, all concussions are a swelling of the brain. The good news in this is that there's no fluid to drain, at least not at this point."

"Has she woken up?"

"No, she has not, and that isn't a bad thing. She needs rest to heal, and that means we have to give her body the support it needs to make that happen. Which is why, thanks to the consent forms you signed, I was able to act quickly and place her in a medically induced coma."

"Coma," I repeat, angry. *Afraid.* "You put her in a fucking coma?" I lower my lashes a moment, tamping down on this wave of anger I didn't invite and irritatingly can't control. My hand lifts, and I look at him. "I'm sorry, Doctor. Please explain."

"A medically induced coma allows us to slow her brain waves, which means the brain needs less energy to heal. And the sooner it heals, the less likely she'll have long-term damage."

"Long-term damage? Do we think—"

"No," he says quickly. "I don't anticipate long-term damage, but that's experience and instinct speaking, not science. The brain is complex, and for all we know about it, we still know much less. I can't promise you an outcome. I can, however, assure you that inducing a coma helps promote a good outcome."

"And you can wake her up from this coma?"

"Yes. It's essentially like having her under anesthesia."

"And the risks in doing this are what?"

"Her blood pressure will be lowered, as will her heart rate, but we've placed a breathing tube and provided the necessary support to ensure she's protected."

"How long will she be like this?"

"I'd expect a week will do the job, but again, that comes from experience, not science. We'll scan again in seventy-two hours. We can't know how her body will react, but we should see improvements by then. For now, sit with her. Talk to her. We're handling this."

Sit. Talk. Wait. Things I'm not good at. Things that don't allow me to fix anything. "And my brother?"

"I know his surgeon well and he's one of the best, not just here, but in the country. Derek's in good hands."

"How long until we know the outcome?"

"I've seen these types of surgeries take two hours and I've seen them take eight. It just depends on what the doctor found when he got in there. The staff here in the private wing is in touch with that team. They'll keep you posted on an hourly basis."

I give a nod. "Thank you, Doctor."

"Hang in there, son." He grabs my shoulder. "We're going to take good care of both of them." He releases me and walks away, but his nurse claims his spot, becoming yet another barrier between me and Emily. "A few instructions are necessary before I leave you alone."

"I'm listening."

"The door to the right of her bed is the entrance to the room where your brother will be after his surgery. We'll update you on his condition every hour and long before he is brought there." She glances at her watch. "I should have an update in another thirty minutes." She lowers her arm and, seeming to understand that I'm not exactly in a chatty mood, moves on without waiting for a reply. "Both rooms have cameras and audio. We can see and hear the monitors from an adjoining booth, but there is also a remote control with a buzzer on the table by her bed. The refrigerator has snacks and the kitchen has coffee. And finally, as tempting as it will be to sit on the bed or hold her, don't. We need to keep her completely still."

"Understood," I bite out, when all I want to do is exactly what she just said: hold Emily and never let her go again.

"Let me know if you need anything," she adds, and once again she doesn't wait for a reply. She steps around me, and her footsteps carry her toward the exit while my gaze lands on Emily. So pale. So unmoving. So lost to me. But her chest rises and falls, her monitor echoing with a steady beat. I want to go to her. I want to pull her into my arms. I want to fucking hold her and never let her go. But I don't. Not yet. I need to be alone with her.

A buzzer sounds, and Seth and I both turn toward the entrance. While Seth walks to the door, I wait, holding my breath for news on Derek. Waiting for what feels like forever, but it is a mere thirty seconds before Seth reappears. "Your clothes," he says, indicating a plastic bag in his hand. "You left them in the bathroom." He crosses to the couch to the left of Emily's bed and tosses the bag onto the coffee table. "The FBI will be handled, by the way. I've already called Nick to get him to call in favors to back this Dennis asshole the hell off."

It's important information. I should care. I don't. "Leave, Seth," I breathe out. "I need to be alone with Emily."

With no discernible reaction, he simply says, "I'll be close," and heads for the door. No ruffled feathers. No politics. No pretense. That's Seth, and if he was any other way right now, it wouldn't end well. His footsteps sound on the floor, echoing like a drum, while my gaze lands on Emily, her face pale. Her brown hair a tangled mess. Her body still so damn unmoving. The doors open and shut, and then there is only the sound of the monitor, and my breathing, which is heavy, thick. I walk to the side of the bed, and my fingers curl into my palms, my need to grab her and kiss her almost too unbearable to contain. I inhale sharply and grab the rolling stool nearby and pull it to the bed, lowering the railing before pulling her cold, tiny hand into mine.

And suddenly I am back in time, remembering the first moment this woman touched my life. Back in the coffee shop of our building.

My order appears and I straighten, intending to claim my coffee and find a seat, when a pretty twentysomething brunette races forward in a puff of sweet, floral-scented perfume, and grabs my coffee.

"Miss," I begin, "that's—"

She takes a sip and grimaces. "What is this?" She turns to the counter and puts it down. "Excuse me!" she calls out. "My drink is wrong."

"Because it's not your drink," Karen reprimands her, setting a new cup on the counter. "This is your drink." She reaches for my cup and turns it around, pointing to the name scribbled on the side. "This one's for Shane." She glances at me. "I'll be right back to fix this. I have another customer."

I wave my acknowledgment and Karen hurries away, while my floral-scented coffee thief faces me, her porcelain cheeks flushed, her full, really damn distracting mouth painted pink. "I'm so sorry," she offers quickly. "I thought I was the only one without my coffee, and I was in a hurry." She starts to hand me my coffee

and then quickly sets it back on the counter. "You can't have that.
I drank out of it."

"I saw that," I say, picking it up. "You grimaced with disgust
after trying it."

Her eyes, a pale blue that matches the short-sleeved silk
blouse she's wearing, go wide. "Oh. I mean no. Or I did, but not
because it's a bad cup of coffee. It's just very strong."

"It's a triple-shot latte."

"A triple," she says, looking quite serious. "Did you know
that in some third world countries, they bottle that stuff and sell
it as a way to grow hair on your chest?" She lowers her voice and
whispers, "That's not a good look for me."

"Fortunately," I say in the midst of a chuckle I would have
claimed wasn't possible five minutes ago, "I don't share that di-
lemma." I lift my cup and add, "Cheers," before taking a drink,
the heavy, rich flavor sliding over my tongue.

She pales, looking exceedingly uncomfortable, before re-
peating, "I drank from that cup."

"I know," I say, offering it back to her. "Try another drink."

She takes the cup and sets it on the counter. "I can't drink
that. And you can't either." She points to the hole on top, now
smudged in pink. "My lipstick is all over it, and I really hate to
tell you this, but it's all over you too and..." She laughs, a soft,
sexy sound, her hands settling on her slender but curvy hips,
accented by a fitted black skirt. "Sorry. I don't mean to laugh, but
it's not a good shade for you."

I laugh now too, officially and impossibly charmed by this
woman in spite of being in the middle of what feels like World
War III. "Seems you know how to make a lasting impression."

"Thankfully it's not lasting," she says. "It'll wipe right off.
And thank you for being such a good sport. I really am sorry
again for all of this."

"Apologize by getting it off me."

Confusion puckers her brow. "What?"

"You put it on me." I grab a napkin from the counter and offer it to her. "You get it off."

"I put it on the cup," she says, clearly recovering her quick wit. "You put it on you."

"I assure you, that had I put it on me, we both would have enjoyed it much more than we are now." I glance at the napkin. "Are you going to help me?"

Her cheeks flush and she hugs herself, her sudden shyness an intriguing contrast to her confident banter. "I'll let you know if you don't get it all."

My apparently lipstick-stained lips curve at her quick wit, but I take the napkin and wipe my mouth, arching a questioning brow when I'm done. She points to the corner of my mouth. "A little more on the left."

I hand her the napkin. "You do it."

She inhales, as if for courage, but takes the napkin. "Fine," she says, stepping closer, that wicked sweet scent of hers teasing my nostrils. Wasting no time, she reaches for my mouth, her body swaying in my direction while my hand itches to settle at her waist. I want this woman and I'm not letting her get away.

"There," she says, her arm lowering.

Not about to let her escape, I capture her hand, holding it and the napkin between us.

Those gorgeous pale blue eyes of hers dart to mine, wide with surprise, the connection sparking an unmistakable charge between us, which I feel with an unexpected but not unwelcome jolt. "Thank you," I say, softening the hard demand in my tone that long ago became natural.

I blink back to the present, with the certainty that I'd fallen in love with her right then, right at that moment. It had been the way she was nervous yet brave. Daring and yet shy. The combination of those things had hinted at the depth of her spirit, the beauty of her character that is so much deeper than the surface beauty, impossible to miss. I glance at the steadiness of the monitor, then at her lowered lashes, and I'd give anything to look into those blue eyes of hers now. "I'm sorry, sweetheart," I whisper. "I should have gotten you out of here. I should have gotten us out of here." I think of my promise to Derek to save the company, but he needs to survive and save it. He will. I won't. "We're going to leave," I promise Emily. "We're going to New York. And I'm going to make every second of every day count."

And it won't matter that Derek can't handle Martina on his own. Martina will be dead.

The thought of killing Martina delivers not anger, not agitation, not pain. It delivers a sense of peace to me that I welcome. It also gives me a sense of control. A sense of direction and focus. I kiss Emily's hand, then kiss her cheek. Then do both again, before I push to my feet and start to pace, plotting the many ways I could, can, and will destroy Martina. The gloves are off. The rules no longer apply. Time ticks by, and I alternate pacing with standing beside Emily, caressing her cheek, checking her monitors. The cycle starts and ends two times before I call the nurse for an update on Derek, which she doesn't have. Another four cycles repeat, and the door to the room buzzes open.

In a rush of energy, Jessica is in the room, hurrying toward me, her newly extended long blonde hair a rumpled mess. "Shane," she breathes out, the lines of her heart-shaped face strained with worry. "Where is she? How is she?" She stops dead in her tracks and stares at the bed. "Oh God." Her hand goes to her head. "Oh God."

I step to her side. "That's how she is."

"Oh God," she says again. "I did this."

"You were drugged."

"Not that badly or I'd be in here like Cody. I was still functioning. I should have followed her to the bathroom when she was sick."

"I should have protected her."

At the sound of Emily's bodyguard's voice, I rotate to find Cody Rodriguez, moving toward us, obviously having entered with Jessica, and while he's dressed in jeans and a T-shirt, his broad shoulders are slumped, his dark complexion pale. "I did this," he repeats, and he is suddenly on a knee.

"Cody!" Jessica shouts, rushing toward him. "You crazy man," she hisses, settling on her jean-clad knee beside him. "You are supposed to be in a hospital bed." She looks at me. "The kidnappers gave him enough of that drug to put down an elephant."

I move to help him, kneeling to take his arm. "Why are you here?"

"She was my responsibility," he says. "I'm her bodyguard."

"You didn't do this," I say. "You need to get back to bed."

"No," he says, shoving to his feet while Jessica and I both follow him, holding on to his arms. "I'm staying with her," he insists. "You don't have to pay me." He pulls away from Jessica and me and walks to the couch beside the bed, where he sits. "I'm staying."

I close the space between us, towering over him. "You need to go get well, Cody."

"I've been worse off than I am now," he assures me, "and I still killed the other guy like I should have tonight." His eyes lock with mine. "I'm your reminder."

My brow furrows with the odd comment. "Reminder?"

"You haven't punched me yet or kicked me out, which means you aren't blaming me. You *don't* own this, but you think you do. And believe me, man. I know how it feels to want to own it. I know that guilt."

I don't blink. I don't react. He doesn't know me and I don't appreciate his attempt to get inside my head, but the very fact that he's here, facing me in his condition when I could blame him, says he's honorable. I'm not sure when this is over if I'll ever be honorable again. I don't feel apologetic for that fact, and I wonder if that's how a person like Martina becomes a person like Martina. Whatever the case, knowing that could well be my path, it doesn't change how much I want and need Emily, who is as pure as snow. Maybe the bad in me just made me selfish, because I have no desire to do right by her and leave her. I just want her. Now. Always. Without the fear of Martina or anyone from her past coming for her. They all have to go. Every last one of them.

"Shane Brandon," Cody says softly, jolting me back to the present, and the moment I refocus on him, he adds, "whatever you think you want to do now, wait a month before you do it. A month gives you time to see it clearly, which you don't right now, I promise you."

I'm not sure if his moral compass is a good thing or a bad thing right about now, and I don't get to make that decision in the moment. The buzzer on the door sounds, and I've instantly dismissed his far too insightful comment, adrenaline roaring through me with the anticipation of news I might not want. Turning toward the door, I find Seth entering the room, accompanied by a short, burly man in scrubs.

"I'm Dr. Ryland," the man announces, offering me his hand,

which I accept, noting the salt and pepper of his thick, neatly trimmed hair, which I hope speaks of experience. "I'm the surgeon who operated on your brother."

Jessica quickly joins us. "How is he?"

"There was a lot of damage to his heart," he says. "But it was also easy to locate and repair, thus why we're already done."

"Which means he'll recover?" I ask cautiously, not yet ready to allow myself hope.

"The next few hours are critical," he says.

"Critical," I repeat. "Meaning he could die at any moment."

"I won't mince words," the doctor says. "Yes. He could die at any time."

Derek could die at any moment. I feel the doctor's announcement like yet another blade cutting through my heart. "And if he makes it through tonight?" I ask. "Then he's out of danger?"

"Really the next few days," the doctor states. "I did my part, but now it's up to his body to do the rest. I'll be in the hospital all night. If he needs me, I'll respond." His phone buzzes, and he pulls it from his pocket to read a message and then glances at me. "He's being rolled into the connecting room now. His wife is already in the room. And I apologize, but I need to respond to another patient in need. I'll check in on him once he's fully settled." He turns to leave, and Seth's brow furrows.

"Wife?" Jessica asks, clearly voicing what Seth and I are both thinking.

"Teresa," I murmur, already turning and walking to the adjoining door, where the next Martina game awaits for me to end, like I plan to end Adrian.

I step into my brother's room, a duplicate of Emily's, and find an empty spot where his bed should be but has yet to arrive. At the entrance, a familiar dark-haired woman standing at the window with her back to the room rotates on a sob, confirming I was right in my assumption of her identity. The "wife" the doctor spoke of is indeed Martina's sister, Teresa.

"I'm sorry," she says, her face swollen from the overflow of tears. "I did this. I knew Ramon was a monster. I should have left sooner. I should have stayed away from Derek."

"You can't be here," I say. "I can't, and won't, have your brother—"

"I forbid him to come here," she says vehemently. "I told him I'd kill him if he came, and I will. I will kill him. He's why any of this could happen. He is why it all happens. He killed my brother. Now. Now , , , now he might have killed "

"No," I say sharply. "Derek is not going to die."

"Do you know something?" she asks hopefully. "Is he okay?"

"He's not okay," I say. "But he is out of surgery. He'll be here any moment."

"Please don't make me leave. I love him," she sobs. "I'm begging you."

I'm thrust back to the memory of being in that ambulance, Derek pleading with me to tell her he loves her. "You can stay."

It's in that moment that a bed is rolled into the room. Seth steps to my side, and Teresa hovers on the other side of the room. In a matter of sixty seconds my brother is the centerpiece of the room, lying in the bed, a tube in his mouth.

"You need to call your parents," Seth says.

"Not yet," I say.

"Shane—"

"Not yet," I bite out. "Not until he wakes up."

And I refuse to believe he won't.

"Shane——"

"When he wakes up," I repeat, refusing to believe he won't. Refusing to accept any outcome but him and Emily walking out of this hospital alive and well. And I don't give Seth time to argue my decision as I step farther into my brother's room to talk to the nurse. From there it's like I'm back in the restaurant, in a tunnel. I watch and listen as she gives me and Teresa, his "wife," instructions. When the nurse leaves, I don't give Teresa time or consideration. I claim a seat next to my brother and I sit down. I talk to him as if he can hear me, when there is nothing to indicate that he can. And finally I stand and face Teresa, wordlessly sizing her up.

"I love him," she repeats, her voice vibrating with emotion. "I'm not leaving without a fight."

I believe her, just as I believe my brother loves her. And he needs a reason to live. Maybe that's her, and for that reason, I can't send her away. That doesn't, however, mean I trust her. She's a Martina who chose to live, work, and exist within the reach of the family business. I can't dismiss that as the problem it represents or the loyalty to a criminal organization it suggests. It's not even like my brother thought otherwise. He wanted to be part of the Martina operation. He accepted being with her as being part of her family. Ultimately that makes her the devil's sister, but I accept her version of evil as tolerable for the moment.

I walk to the door, where Seth waits, or rather, stands guard. At my approach, he disappears into the next room, and I pause in the archway between the adjoining rooms, speaking to Teresa without turning to face her. "Leave the door open," I order, and I don't wait for an answer.

I enter Emily's room, and I swear a knot of emotion forms in my chest with the familiar scent in the room that is her. Every part of me wants to turn to her, to go to her, but I know with absoluteness that if I look at her right now, some part of me will shatter, and I don't know how and where those pieces will land. With Herculean effort, I instead hone in on Cody, who is now on the opposite side of the room, sprawled out on the couch in the living area, a gun on the coffee table beside him, his hand on it.

"Does his medical staff know he's here?" I ask as Seth steps in front of me.

"I'll make sure they do."

"What can I do?" Jessica asks, joining us.

"Go home and rest," I say, unwilling to answer the questions I know she'll soon ask.

"I'm staying," she says.

"You're not staying," I reply.

"Emily's my friend. *You're* my friend."

"I'm your boss," I amend. "Go home."

"Shane—"

"You're a smart woman, Jessica," I say. "You know there are things going on here that don't exactly smell good. And thus, you have to know you could be in one of these beds tonight. Don't argue and don't ask questions I'm not going to answer."

"I can handle this," she says. "Whatever it is, I can handle it."

"I don't want you to handle it," I reply. "I want you to go home."

Her expression tightens, that stubbornness I know in her brimming from her eyes. "People are going to ask me questions."

"Send them to me," Seth offers.

She looks like she wants to argue, but she manages a

tight-lipped "fine" in reply. "I'll leave. I'll dodge and weave questions. For now. But I'm involved. I want answers, and I'll be back early with a change of clothes for you, and for Emily, when she wakes up." She turns and walks away, Seth on her heels, while my mind is on her reference to questions she might ask, on top of Seth's reference to my parents. I need answers of my own. I fish my phone from my pocket and key in Martina's number.

Martina's line rings at the same moment the door slams shut with Jessica's departure. He answers in one ring with, "I understand my sister is there."

"Alive and well," I say, "unlike my brother and my woman. How well is this situation contained?"

"Completely," he states. "Derek and Emily had a car accident while being driven by a car service, and the driver will back that story up fully. Details are in a folder being delivered to your man Seth. Coincidentally, there was a break-in at my restaurant tonight that ended in tragedy."

"What happened to the jealous lover story?"

"It places them at my restaurant."

"And what's going to hit the press?"

"The robbery," he states. "The car accident is fully suppressed. When and how you tell people your situation is on you."

I don't ask how he's coordinated this with medical and law enforcement involved. I end the call at the same moment Seth returns. "The press isn't an issue," I say, relaying the call details.

"I'll look at the information he sends us and confirm we're covered," Seth replies when I've finished. "And if it checks out, you have some time with the stockholders, and your parents, but you don't have a lot of time here, Shane."

"We hired Nick and his team for a reason," I say. "They need to make sure I have whatever time I decide I need. Including containing Agent Dennis."

He gives me a several-second unreadable stare before he says, "I'll handle it," and then changes the subject. "What do you want to do about your unexpected visitor?"

Understanding his meaning, I glance at Cody, who still lies dead to the world on the living room couch—but that hand of his remains on his gun, ready to act. "Leave him," I say. "He can sit with Teresa when he's well."

Cody sits up, swaying and a little green, to announce, "I'll do it now" before standing up and, with remarkable speed, considering how drugged and violently ill he was only hours before, walks toward us and I watch as he continues on to my brother's room.

"You don't blame him, or Nick's team, for Emily's kidnapping," Seth says.

"Blaming other people is an escape we give ourselves, which I don't want, or need, right now."

He narrows his eyes on me, looking beneath the surface of my answer, and while I have no idea what it is he finds, the slight darkening of his eyes tells me he doesn't like it. But to his credit, and good sense, he leaves it alone. "I'll get to work on our cover story, and should it check out, ensure everyone, Jessica included, is using it. Consider it done, unless you hear otherwise." At my nod, he adds, "I'll be in the building," before he turns and starts walking toward the door.

I stand there, listening to his footsteps, inhaling the sweet, floral scent of Emily that not even blood and bullets has erased. She is sweetness. She is perfection. She is the light in the darkness that I can find nowhere else. The door opens and shuts, and finally I am alone with the woman I love, and every hole this

night has created and every emotion it's stirred have had time
to settle into those now hollow places.

Inhaling again, I rotate, walking to the end of Emily's
hospital bed. My gaze lands on her face, that damn tube in
her mouth. My eyes lower and I'm back in another memory:

*I'm pulling my tie from my neck and standing before her
panties ever hit the ground. "I'm going to tie you up, Emily," I
say, closing the small space between us to tower over her.*

*Her response is quick and unexpected. "On one condition,"
she says.*

*"I'm listening," I say, and suddenly, while waiting on her
answer, I realize she might be without clothes, but I am naked in
every other possible way. And I know then that I am fucked up
tonight, both looking for her confession of fear and dreading it.*

*"When this is over, you will not question how or why it hap-
pened. This is my choice. You didn't intimidate me into saying
yes. You didn't scare me. I chose to give you this control because
I trust you. Because I am not afraid of you, and when you are like
you are tonight, I still won't be." She offers me her hands.*

*Every nerve in my body is jumping. Every dark part of me is
now on fire. Every emotion is a twisted knot that torments me
with a demand that it be named. I won't allow myself that kind of
weakness, and the theme of this night returns: anger. Emily is the
one pushing me to feel these things. She is the one pushing me to
prove one thing: that I didn't see what I saw in her eyes tonight.*

*I toss the tie away and drag her to me, tangling fingers in
her hair again and cupping her backside. "Denial is destructive.
You know that, right?"*

*"I do," she says, her fingers on my chest. "I know, but do
you?"*

*"Damn it, Emily," I growl, my mouth coming down on hers,
my tongue sliding past her lips, a band of tension wrapping*

around us, my need to bend her will, to force her to admit the truth, dominating, the way I want to dominate her. But she doesn't let me dominate her.

Her kiss is as fierce as mine. Her tongue as demanding, while her soft little hand manages to slide under my shirt, which is somehow untucked, and scorch my skin. I deepen the kiss and squeeze her backside again, not sure who is pushing whom. Not finding the fear I'd sought or expected, and that drives me to want it, to want her, all the more. I raise my hand and give her a smack on the bottom just hard enough to get her attention.

She yelps and then pants into my mouth. "Was that supposed to scare me? Because it didn't." She pulls back and looks at me, no hesitation in her words or eyes. "In fact, it turns me on. Everything with you turns me on, Shane. Do it again."

Possessiveness rises hard and fast, unfamiliar and intense. "Who spanked you before me?"

"Nothing matters before you," she says, her fingers curling at my jawline. "Do it again. You want to. I feel it. I know it."

"Holy fuck, woman. I was worried about scaring you."

"You mean you were convinced I was already scared. I wasn't and you can't scare me, but you can piss me off like you did when Martina left. That wasn't fear you saw in my eyes, Shane. That was anger. I was pissed. I still am."

I don't do us the injustice of pretending to be naive. "Because I didn't want you to hear that meeting."

"Yes," she says. "And you know my past and all the secrets and lies. You know the lie I have to live to survive. Don't give me more of the same."

"I also know the reasons your family gave you to feel insecure. I don't want you to feel that."

"Secrets make me feel that."

"It's not about secrets. I was—"

"Don't say 'protecting me' again. Don't even say it. Even now you want to be the person you were in that elevator, and you won't. Give me everything or nothing. I can't do in-between. So you want to fuck me, you want to spank me? Stop holding back." She grabs my shirt. *"Stop holding things back from me. I want the good, bad, and ugly. I want—"*

I kiss her again, and damn it, if she wants the bad and the ugly, I'll give them to her. I lift her and carry her to the couch, sitting down, and before she even knows my intention, I have her over my lap, my hand on her backside. "I'm going to spank you now."

"Do it," she hisses. "Do it now."

I blink back to the present, and while some might see this as an oddly timed memory, I do not. To me it's about the many intimate things we've shared. About the many layers there are to this woman, layers I have only just begun to discover, when I want to know them all. It's about how she challenges me and forbids me to hide from me. It's about strength. Hers. Mine. Ours together. It's about how fucking much I need her to wake up and challenge me again and again and again.

I grab the railing in front of me. "I need you, Emily," I whisper, and still she doesn't move. Still she is just lying there, barely living. My head lowers, my chin at my chest, and I swear I can't even catch my breath right now.

CHAPTER FOUR

I don't know how long I stand at the foot of Emily's bed. Five minutes. Thirty. A full hour. But my body is stiff, and my mind is a muddy black hole, where everything is lost but not found. I push off the bed, intending to check on my brother, but for several beats my gaze lingers on Emily, some part of me needing to watch that breathing machine lift her chest one more time. Inhale. Exhale. I force myself to turn away, and when I do, a new urgency forms inside me, my need to confirm my brother's safety carrying me to the open door dividing this room from his.

Stepping under the archway, I find Derek as expected, still in a bed in the center of the room, still with tubes and machines connected to him. What I don't expect is Teresa sitting beside him, talking to him in muffled words I cannot make out, though I suspect that Cody is another story. He sits behind her, in a leather chair in the corner, his complexion still pretty damn green, but his eyes are on me, his stare meeting mine, the silent message clear: he's here. He's aware. He has control despite the hell his body has been through tonight. He blames himself, as anyone in his role whould, even when that blame is misplaced, as his is.

My gaze shifts back to Teresa, who abruptly looks up, her attention rocketing to me, uncertainty in her eyes. The kind you want to keep in the eyes of a Martina. The kind I don't want to have about my brother's future, but there is nothing I can do right now that will change that fact. He's still unconscious. He's still not breathing on his own. And so I settle for what I can do, and that's keeping Teresa on edge, where she belongs.

I turn away from her and leave the room, reentering Emily's, and this time I go right to her. I need to be by her side and know that we are alone. My need for revenge, and the necessity that I ensure everyone who caused this pays a price, fades into the background. There is just Emily, and I pull a chair to the edge of her bed and sit down. With her hand in mine, I start talking to her about anything and everything. About the past, present, and future. About my parents. About her family. About the Brandon fashion brand she aspired to start and I want to watch her build. But most of all, I tell her how much I need her. I tell her how much I want her. I even talk about kids I didn't think I wanted until I sit with her and realize how much this world needs more of her.

At some point, I fall asleep, because I wake with my head resting on Emily's bed, and a nurse needing me to move so she can check Emily's vitals. "My brother?" I ask, stepping out of her way.

"No change."

And so it goes for the next few hours. I sit with Emily. I check on Derek. I pace. And eventually, for sanity reasons, my brain starts to work on my plans for the future. I hate Martina.

I want to destroy him. I want to kill him, but his family is after our pharmaceutical brand, and our stockholder Mike Rogers wants my mother to stay in his bed while he claims our company. That isn't going to happen. I have to finish my plan to shut them both down. Sell Mike the pharmaceutical brand and let Martina be his nightmare. A deal he has until Monday to take, and he will. With that deal sealed, I will move on to buy the sports complex where Mike's team plays, with Adrian's consortium as investors, to give Adrian control over Mike. It's sweet revenge on Mike. And it's a sweet deal for Adrian that gets him out of our company and our lives. Too sweet for that bastard, but I'll deal with him later.

My mind works, my plans taking hold, and once the reasonable hour of five in the morning arrives, I send a text message to Jessica and arrange to have my work, along with my MacBook, brought to me. By the time Emily and Derek are out of the hospital, I will have purged our company of the poison that is Mike Rogers and Adrian Martina. But the purge won't be complete, I think, and my mind goes to Teresa sitting next to my brother's bed. Adrian will use her and my brother's feelings for her to retain a connection to me and our company, if I let him, which I won't. And if my brother survives this, I'll be damned if I allow her to be the demise he's avoided. She left once. She has to leave again.

But she doesn't leave.

At least not over the next few days, and not by the time Wednesday morning arrives. She stays by Derek's side, and Cody stays by hers. That is, until thirty minutes ago, when they kicked him and her out of Derek's room to give Derek a sponge bath and medications. Cody joins me right about the time Emily is taken back for a new CT scan. "What's taking so damn long?" I demand, pacing the room, when I was never a pacer before this room consumed my life and everyone I love.

"They just took her back," Cody replies. He glances at his watch from where he leans on the kitchen counter, a bag of M&M's in his hand. He sports the same thick stubble on his jaw that I do. "Fifteen minutes ago. They told us forty-five minutes to an hour."

I glance at my watch to confirm. "Right." My lips thin. "An hour." Frustrated, my hands settle on my hips, my clean jeans and T-shirt compliments of Jessica, as I suspect are Cody's, since he's yet to leave the building. "Where did Teresa go when they ran you out of the room?"

"According to our team watching her," he says, "the coffee shop on the first floor. And that's the farthest from his side she's been in days."

"And yours," I say, sitting on the arm of the living area couch facing him. "What's your take on Teresa?"

"She's guarded," he says. "Which isn't unexpected considering she was born into the Martina cartel, but it does tell me that she's learned to navigate that role. That doesn't mean she embraces it, but she's not as sweet and pure as she tries to seem."

"Is she using my brother for a Martina agenda?"

"I don't know how her motivation started," he says. "But no. That woman loves your brother. And before you ask how I know, I see it in her eyes. I hear it in her voice and in the many tears she's shedding. The woman hasn't left his side. She was reading him *Hunger Games* this morning."

"*Hunger Games,*" I repeat. "Just what I need. My brother being read a book on war games while lying in a bed as a victim of what amounts to war games."

"Yeah," he says. "I didn't miss that irony either, but despite that choice, she wanted him to hear her voice."

My phone rings and I fish it from my pocket, eyeing the screen to find my caller is Mike Rogers, who's right on time, considering his deadline to accept the deal to split the company. I ignore the call, having no intentions of talking to him until after I have Emily back in the room safe and secure, and I have the new details I need to seal the deal to buy the sports center, where Rogers's basketball team plays. Which will be soon. Really damn soon.

The buzzer sounds to the door, and I'm on my feet in an instant, adrenaline rushing through me, followed by disappointment at the sight of Jessica, who looks a bit too funeral-ready in a black pantsuit. "Good grief," she chides. "Don't look so upset to see me. I brought the documents you wanted and as a bonus"—she stops a few feet from me, indicating the tray in her hand—"coffee."

"Documents and coffee are good," I say. "Surprises right now are not."

"Right." She shoves her blonde hair behind her ear and gives a nervous glance toward the empty bedroom. "I really hate not seeing her there, but I knew she was having her CT scan this morning. I'm sorry. I should have warned you I was coming up."

"Sorry?" I ask. "You, Jessica, said you're sorry?"

"I'm not an asshole, Shane Brandon. You know, maybe this triple shot I got you is a bad idea. You're wired in all the wrong ways."

Cody pushes to his feet and takes the tray from her. "Never threaten a sleep-deprived man's coffee. It's dangerous."

"Tired is the point," she tells him. Then, refocusing on

me, she adds, "You need sleep, not caffeine. I should have seen that. I'll stay and sit with Derek and Emily while you rest and shave your hairy face." She glances at Cody. "Both of you need to use a razor." She doesn't give us time to argue, turning to me again. "You will be worthless for Derek and Emily if they wake up." She pales. "When. When they wake up."

The "if" guts me. "When," I bite out, accepting the coffee Cody hands me, hoping like hell that day is today for both of them. "And when they do, that's when I'll get some rest."

"In other words, I can't win this argument," she says.

"No," I say. "You cannot."

"Do I dare ask about Derek?" she asks, accepting a cup of coffee from Cody, who claims the arm of the couch.

"He's unchanged," I say.

"Which means what?" she presses.

"Still unconscious," Cody supplies.

She glances between him and me. "Is that expected, considering his injuries?"

"The standard reply to that question is 'he's stable,'" Cody replies.

"That isn't an answer," she says.

"Exactly," I say with a bitter laugh I wash down with a swig of my coffee. "That's what I keep saying, but stable is a hell of a lot better than not."

"What about Emily?" she asks. "What are they saying about her progress?"

"She's as expected while in an induced coma," I say. "They can't tell us more until after this test."

"Which is why you're a live wire," she says. "Whatever they say after this test, you have to get some rest, Shane. I can stay the night and sit with Emily while you rest a few hours."

"Nothing has changed," I say. "I want you far away from this."

She glances between me and Cody. "From the car accident," she says.

"Yes," Cody says, his eyes meeting hers. "From the car accident."

"That wasn't a car accident," she challenges, and there is a vibe between these two, something that screams personal and potentially a problem I don't need right now.

"I need that paperwork, Jessica," I say, walking to the bar I've set up as a workstation and setting my coffee down.

"Right," she says, joining me and allowing the oversized bag on her shoulder to settle on the counter. "Twelve documents," she says, setting a folder on the desk.

I grab a pen, open the folder, and start inking my name. "Have them delivered by courier today for countersignatures and set the countdown clock. Each investor has seventy-two hours to fund their portion of the buyout of the complex, or they're out."

"Got it." Her cell phone rings and she digs it out of her purse. "Mike Rogers. I don't even know how he got my number, but he's called me three times this morning."

"Ignore him," I say, finishing off the documents, and then I shut the folder.

"And if he comes to the office?"

"Tell him I'm negotiating a financial win for us all and I'll be in touch soon."

The door buzzes and I'm on my feet in an instant, watching as Emily is rolled back into the room. "Get those documents out," I order Jessica, already moving forward to follow the nursing team of two as they reposition Emily's bed.

"Where do we stand?" I ask, taking up a post at the foot of the bed.

"The doctor will be in to talk to you in just a moment," one of the nurses informs me.

"Define a moment," I say.

"Right now." I turn to find the doctor approaching. "And right now I have good news. The swelling in her brain is re-solving nicely. We're going to wake her up."

The rush of relief I feel in that moment is impossible to explain, like a vise that releases my airways and allows me to draw in air. "How do we wake her up? What happens next?"

"We'll gradually reduce the medication and the support from the breathing machine we're giving her," he says. "By this evening we should be able to take out the breathing tube."

"When will she be aware of her surroundings?"

"This isn't an event, but rather a process," he says. "Even when she seems to be awake, she'll likely be groggy and not fully aware of what is happening around her."

"Are we sure she's going to wake up?"

"I know you're worried, son," he says. "And with the brain, we can never be certain, but I'm expecting a positive out-come. You should too." He eyes one of the nurses and gives her instructions to lower Emily's medication and oxygen, before looking at me again. "I'm in the hospital all day. I'll be looking out for her." He pats my shoulder and heads for the door.

Cody, in turn, claims his spot, stepping to my side. "I got the all clear to head back into your brother's room, and Teresa is already there. If you need me, I'm a shout away." He doesn't wait for the reply I wasn't going to give, already mov-ing away, while I myself am focused on Emily, waiting impa-tiently until the nurses give me room to claim the seat next to her.

The instant they are gone, I'm by her side, drawing her hand into mine. "Time to come back to me, sweetheart. I need you to come back now." I lean over her and kiss her cheek, then repeat what I've been telling her for days: "I need you, Emily. I love you."

The buzzer sounds, and I glance up to find Seth striding toward us, clearly in work mode, in a gray suit and matching tie, his jaw set hard. "We have a problem."

"Save it," I say. "Right now we're waking up Emily."

"Mike Rogers is in the lobby," he announces, stopping at the end of the bed.

"How does Mike Rogers know we're here?"

"My best guess is that he followed Jessica. Bottom line: he's here. He's in the main lobby, insisting that he sees you."

As much as I want to send the man away, sealing the deal to split the company only helps me ensure that when Emily wakes up, I can promise her changes are in place. I force myself to release Emily's hand and push to my feet. "Stay with Emily," I order Seth, and I don't wait for a reply.

Ready to end Mike Rogers as a business partner, a problem I need to deal with today, I stride around the bed and to the door, exiting into the hallway and wasting no time making my way to the elevators. I've just punched the call button when the doors open and, lo and behold, Mike, who shouldn't be allowed on this floor, appears.

"Shane," he greets me, his voice as hard as his square jaw is solid.

I don't greet him and I don't ask how he's gotten in here. Staying close to Emily and Derek suits me just fine, and I back up, giving him room to enter the corridor. He exits the car, his fitted, expensive suit a tan color I'd never choose, but then, there is nothing much the two of us agree on.

"I need to speak to your father before I sign this paper-work," he states.

"My father's in Germany and I'm legally in control."

"Stop the bullshit," he says. "You wouldn't be here in this hospital if he were being treated in Germany."

Realization hits me. "You don't know."

"Apparently there's a lot I don't know. That's why your father and I—"

"Derek and Emily were in a car accident Sunday night," I say.

His eyes go wide. "What? Holy fuck. How bad?"

"Bad. And my parents don't know and won't know until I can tell them that Derek's regained consciousness. That means, while you're conspiring with my mother to destroy my father, keep your mouth shut."

"I'm not conspiring with your mother."

"Just fucking her," I say. "Right. Got it." I move on. "What-ever you want to know about the offer I gave you, ask me. My father doesn't even know about it."

Surprise flashes in his eyes. "And if he objects?"

"The deal will be done."

"Why give me the most profitable part of the company?"

"Buying and selling for a profit is a profit for me. And I'm leaving this with a profit for my portion of the company. I'm leav-ing you with an empire. The basketball team owner who rules the pharmaceutical industry. And when my father recovers, and he will, he's kept the side of the business he loves and created in the hedge fund operation. And my mother. He keeps my mother. Sign the deal, Mike. It's a win for all of us, and we both like to win."

He studies me for several drawn-out beats before he reaches into his pocket and hands me an envelope. "The contract," he says, "and my lawsuit will be withdrawn before day's end."

"And my mother?"

"We haven't spoken in weeks and we won't in the future."

I'd ask for his word, but I wouldn't trust it anyway. The file of nastiness I have on him sure to turn my mother against him is another story. I accept the document and open my mouth to speak, when voices lift behind us and some sort of alarm goes off. I have no idea why, but those sounds register like a knife in my chest. I rotate toward them and see nothing, but I hear it. I feel it, whatever it is. Dread. Fear. Foreboding. I start running toward the private wing I've just left, adrenaline rushing through me, blood rushing in my ears, because I know, I just know, that death is here to stake a claim, and it's not going to leave without someone I love.

CHAPTER FIVE

Two weeks have passed. Two weeks since death visited that hospital and refused to leave without someone I loved.

I grip the cold steel of my apartment's balcony railing, memories pounding on me, filling the dark space of a darker midnight hour with a replay of that moment when I knew my life would forever be changed. When I knew *I'd* forever be changed. Over and over, I see the medical staff scrambling. Over and over, their shouts and that damn alarm filling the air play in my head, echoing in the quiet hollows of downtown Denver, along with a low rumble of thunder somewhere in the not so far distance.

I blink away the images that try to form, bloody, horrible images of the restaurant that are as bad, if not, worse, than those moments in the hospital room. But I fail to erase them, and in the inky black of a starless night, I can almost see blood-stained clouds. Suddenly I am back in Martina's restaurant, blood on my hands, blood everywhere. I just keep going back there, holding the holes in my brother's chest shut while Emily lay several feet away, alone on the hard floor. And each time, I remember Martina standing over us, the man who ultimately motivated every action my brother and Ramon took to get us to that miserable moment. And that's when I return to my vow to punish Martina and kill him. I want to punish him even more than I want to kill him.

A loud crash sounds somewhere on the street, and I blink back to the present, my gaze seeking out the source of that noise to find nothing but more darkness. But somewhere down there someone maneuvered wrong, right when it should have been left, or too soon, or too slow. Like I maneuvered wrong, or none of this would have happened. I should have taken Emily to New York. I should have made Derek listen. I should have done so many fucking things differently. But no, I was cocky. I knew what I was doing. I knew I was the real king, not my father.

Scrubbing my jaw, I step back into the dim glow of the barely there lights on the patio, my skin icy beneath my white T-shirt and pajama bottoms, but the cold is better than the pain. And still it doesn't stop me from picturing the paramedics leaning over Derek and Emily, the intense looks on their faces as they worked to save their lives. Desperate to get the images out of my head, I pull my phone from my pocket and turn on the radio to a pop station sure to have meaningless lyrics playing, needing anything but my thoughts in my head. Once some bouncing, ridiculous tune is playing, I walk to the table and sit down under the overhead heater I haven't bothered to turn on.

The music changes, and a song I know from college starts to play. "Collide," I think it's called, and I rest my elbows on my legs, lowering my chin to rest on my chest, the words of the song overtaking me. My chest and eyes burn with those lyrics, and I am immediately remembering the tormented moment outside of the restaurant as Derek and Emily were rolled toward two separate ambulances. When I'd been forced to choose between them. When Eric had convinced me to choose Derek, that Emily was stable, and yet I feared I'd never see Emily again. Some part of me knew even then that my heart was going to be ripped out before it was all over.

Inhaling sharply, I lift my head and reach for the whiskey glass on the table next to me, downing what remains inside, which apparently is nothing. Nothing is fucking left. Until I hear my name. "Shane."

Emily's voice.

It reaches me above the music, and I inhale softly as the delicate notes slide into the deep black hole of my soul and make it just a little lighter. And when I draw in a breath, a familiar soft floral scent touches my nostrils.

Emily's scent.

I can smell her. I can almost taste her, but almost isn't real. Maybe it's not Emily here at all. Maybe it's just me, needing her until it hurts. Afraid it's true, I shut my eyes again, and I savor her scent. I imagine her long, dark hair on her face, on mine. Warmth rushes over me, and I look up to find the heater above me glowing. The air shifts then, and Emily steps in front of me, a sheer white silk gown clinging to her slender body, her long, dark hair that I'd just been imagining lifting in the air. That sweet floral scent that had been taunting me moments before, taunting me again, promising she is real. She stands there, a sway from leaning into me, an untouchable angel, a piece of my dreams, which is why I don't reach for her. I don't want her to be my imagination. I don't want to know that she's not real. I don't want to know that if she is real, I have a chance to destroy her all over again. The way that night in the restaurant destroyed me.

"Shane," she says again, this time her voice a barely there whisper.

My lashes lift, and indeed she's still here, still beautiful. Still everything I greedily need and can't even imagine letting go. Her eyes soften, as if she's read some part of my thoughts that even I may not understand. I'm not sure that is good or bad, considering some of the places my mind has gone these past few days. But I'm not hiding from her. I tried that once. I failed.

She lifts her arm, and my chest expands on a breath of anticipation. A moment later her palm settles on my cheek, and her touch is like a cool breeze in the burning hell I am now trapped inside. I am not worthy of her, and yet I find myself leaning into her touch, squeezing my eyes shut tighter in a conflicted moment of absorption and certainty that when I open them again, she will no longer be here. That idea spikes an emotion in me I can call only one thing: fear. Memories of her in a hospital bed, tormenting my mind: tubes and machines connected to her. Me watching her chest for its rise and fall despite the monitors telling me she was breathing.

My hand goes to hers, covering it on my jaw. My eyes reopen, fixing her in a stare. "Tell me you're real."

"You know I'm real."

My arm wraps around her waist, and I pull her onto my lap, her legs straddling my hips in the wide cushioned chair I occupy, warmth beaming over us from the heater above. Our heads coming together, and for long moments, maybe even a full minute or more, we just breathe each other in. "I need . . ." I begin.

"Me too," she finishes, and I know she's struggling as I am. She was attacked. Captive. In a coma, and she woke up to a world turned upside down. She was supposed to be safe with me. I was supposed to protect her, and on that, I also failed.

"Emily," I whisper, for no other reason than I just want her on my lips, on my tongue, in every possible way.

"I'm here," she breathes out, dragging her gown over her head and tossing it aside, leaving herself naked but for her panties, her breasts high, her nipples pebbled. Her body is perfection to me and yes, I am instantly hard. Yes, I want to be inside her, but nothing about this moment or night is about sex or fucking. It's about that need we spoke of that cannot even be fully quantified or explained. It just is, and as I drag Emily closer, my hand finds the spot between her shoulder blades and I mold her to me. Holding her too tight and yet not tight enough as my mind replays her screams when I entered that restaurant, before that moment when shots were fired and a bloody hell followed. "That night . . ." I begin.

"I don't remember," she says. "I really don't."

I believe her, and I'm not sure if that's a gift or a curse. "Just know this," I say. "I will never let you get hurt again. I will never let anyone touch you but me, and if they try, I swear to God above, I'll kill them."

"No," she says, her fingers curling into my T-shirt as she pulls back to look at me. "Don't do that to yourself or me. You can't protect me from everything and everyone, and that's not what I want from you."

I tangle my fingers in her hair, dragging her lips a brush from mine. "I can and I will," I say, sealing that vow with a kiss, my mouth closing over hers, my tongue sliding into her mouth in a deep caress, followed by another, the taste of her bittersweet in ways I wish I could erase. She moans, a soft, sweet sound that vibrates on my tongue, but just as she melts into me, a sudden downpour of rain and hail jolts us apart, our mouths lingering close, and it's like the storm sets off an eruption between us. One minute we are sitting there, listening to the thunder of the hail against the railing behind us, the next our mouths come together again, and this time we aren't just kissing. We are drinking each other in, consuming each other, and yet we seem to be incapable of getting enough of some unnamed critical something that is all part of that need we expressed.

She reaches for my shirt and starts tugging it upward. I answer her action by tearing my mouth from hers, dragging it over my head and tossing it aside. It's barely gone when her fingers are in my hair, her lips on mine again. Her hands on my skin, touching, caressing, while mine are on hers, and I can feel the burn of some dark emotion inside me turning to lust. Driven by that emotion, I reach down and rip away Emily's panties, swallowing her soft, sexy gasp, the slide of her tongue against mine, fuel to the lust raging inside me, thickening my cock.

Lifting her, I feel one of us maneuver my pants—me, her, I really don't know or care—until she is sliding down the thick pulse of my erection, taking me inside her. And once she has, we don't linger there either. We don't savor the moment she has all of me. There is still that need between us, ravishing, demanding satisfaction, and we answer with the sway of our bodies, the licks of our tongues. The frenzied grind of hips against hips. We're wild. We're lost in each other, the sound of hail and rain mingling with the pants and sighs of pleasure until I hear her panted, "Shane," and feel her body tense with her release, her sex gripping my shaft as surely as her fingers tug on my hair. And I'm right there with her, riding the wave of her release right into mine, my body quaking with her body. Time fades. The hell of the past few weeks disappears. There is just this woman who I love, who I need to protect and love some more.

We collapse together, her soft curves against the hard lines of my body, which doesn't relax. I'm not sure I'll ever relax again. But holding her like this, having her close, her breath warm on my shoulder, telling me she's alive and well, this is the closest thing to peace I've felt in weeks. That is, until I hear her sob. I shift her, cupping her face, and bring her gaze to mine, my thumbs stroking tears from her eyes. "Talk to me."

"I remember now. I don't know what about this moment jolted my memory. Maybe it's your emotions feeding mine, but I *remember*. God. I remember him throwing himself on top of me, Shane. I remember Derek protecting me." Her hands go to my wrist. "Shane. He died protecting me. It's my fault."

"No. No, this not your fault," I say. "You didn't make him get involved with Martina. You didn't do this."

"He was protecting me," she says.

"And he wanted you to survive. That's the first thing he asked me in the ambulance. Were you okay. He wanted you to be okay."

She presses her hands to her face. "Oh God. Derek."

I grab my shirt from the floor and pull out of her before pressing it between her legs, righting my pajamas, and then scooping her up. She curls against my chest, the dampness of her tears touching my skin, and I carry her inside, shutting the patio door and heading toward the bedroom. In a few seconds I've climbed the stairs and entered our bedroom, the light a dim glow from the lamp on her nightstand, while mine remains off. I settle her on the bed, and while I intend to lie down with her, she is quick to sit up, sliding to the edge of the bed.

"I hate what I'm feeling right now," she says, her words and actions telling me that she feels as naked inside as out right now.

I grab the blanket at the end of the mattress and wrap it around her, settling on a knee in front of her. "You didn't do this," I say. "You are not to blame."

"Says the man who has done nothing but blame himself since I woke up from my coma?" She laughs without humor. "Coma. I was in a coma."

"But you're alive and well now."

"Because of Derek," she says. "The funeral's in a few days, Shane. How do I face your parents when they arrive for the funeral, knowing it was him or me and it ended up being me?"

"My parents are the ones who should be afraid to face us and themselves in the mirror," I say, anger spiking in me hard and fast. "My father pushed Derek to do anything to succeed while my mother plotted against him to ensure she was on the arm of Mike Rogers when he claimed control of the company."

"You don't understand, Shane," she says, her voice quaking. "I *remember* now. I remember the moment when a gun was pointed at me and when Derek threw himself in front of me. He selflessly *threw himself* in front of me and a bullet. I'd be dead right now if not for him."

"And if there is a heaven and a hell, and I believe there is, you are the reason he's not burning in hell. You became the vehicle that let the brother I knew and loved but thought was lost be discovered again. That brother would always put someone else before himself."

"If he was willing that night, he was always willing," she says. "He was always that person. Had I left when I tried to leave, and stayed out of his life and yours, he might have walked out of there that night alive. I complicated the situation. I should not have inserted myself into your lives."

"That's nothing but survivor's guilt talking," I say. "And I'm pretty sure there have been books written on it. It's natural to blame yourself, but you *are not* to blame. He was in bed with a drug lord, ready to get deeper under the covers. That doesn't exactly spell long life."

"Part of me wishes I wouldn't have remembered what happened," she whispers. "Another part knows he deserves to have me remember."

"He deserves to have us remember," I agree.

"But your parents—"

"Don't need to know," he says. "It wouldn't matter to them."

"He was a hero in the end," she says. "As his parents—"

"It *won't matter* to them, Emily," I say, my voice as hard as the reality behind the words.

"Do you really believe that?"

"Yes," I say without hesitation. "I do, and I know you know it's true."

"I *don't* know," she says. "And I want you to be wrong."

"They both used him, and me for that matter, in their own ways, on their own terms. I had to wait to tell my father that Derek was dead until after he told me he was in remission. Even Derek's funeral has to wait for their return home."

"I know," she says. "I hate that, but I'm back to being conflicted. Part of me is glad we have to wait because it means I don't have to accept he's gone. The other part thinks he deserves to be put to rest. And I know from losing my father and mother that, really, you don't start healing until after the funeral. It's when you start finding closure. When you start working toward some kind of peace."

This is where she wants me to agree, even expects it, but I don't. "Let's try to rest."

"On one condition," she says. "You don't leave, Shane."

She's not talking about now. She's talking about the bigger picture, the fear of losing the ones you love that death has a way of creating. "I'm not leaving you and you aren't leaving me."

"Of course we can't promise each other that," she says. "But somehow saying it makes it feel more real, doesn't it?"

"We aren't going to lose each other," I promise. "Come on." I maneuver us both into the bed and under the covers, with her snuggled close to my side. Neither of us moves to turn out the light and, at least for me, the darkness is somehow a place more empty than it once had been.

I hold Emily, and I think of her words about the funeral: *It's when you start finding closure. When you start working toward some kind of peace.* She is right. Those things are coming, but not with, or because of, the funeral. They're coming with, and because of, the justice I'm going to deliver for my brother.

CHAPTER SIX

Morning comes with me still awake, staring at the ceiling and listening to Emily breathe, while I remind myself how close I came to losing her, as I have Derek. At the first light of Saturday morning, careful not to wake her, I slip out of the bed and into the closet. Once inside, I bypass the suits and ties I haven't worn for weeks to snap up a pair of sweats and a T-shirt. I'm about to exit when my gaze returns to those suits, and I think about choosing one for the funeral. I have to choose a suit to bury my brother, and I find myself back in that ambulance, holding his hand as he said, "Save the company."

"Damn it, Derek," I hiss, my fingers curling into my palms. "I told you we were going to do it together. We were *supposed* to do it together. That's what I always wanted." I shake myself, mentally and even physically, before exiting the closet, to find myself pausing, staring at Emily where she rests in the bed. In *our* bed, in our home, where I intend to keep her safe, no matter what I have to do to ensure that happens. With that thought driving me, I'm ready to get to work sealing every loose end in our lives right now, and I cross to the bathroom, shut the door, and make my shower fast, in hopes Emily won't hear the water.

Fully dressed, I step to the sink to shave, not because it's necessary, but because I want control in all things right now. I will never lose control again, like I did two weeks ago. I lather up and take the blade to my face, precise in my strokes, the way I plan to be about every move I make to get to that peace and closure Emily mentioned last night and beyond, to the justice I seek and will have. When I'm done, I head to the bedroom to find her standing up and knotting the sash of her pink silk robe, her dark hair a tousled, sexy mess.

"Hey," she says.

"Hey, sweetheart," I say, closing the distance between us and pulling her close, my palms settling at her neck, under her hair. "How's your head today? We didn't overdo things for you last night, did we?"

"Things?" She laughs, her hands settling at my waist. "No. We did not overdo *things*. I'm officially off bed rest now, and I don't even have a headache this morning. But it is kind of scary how deeply I'm sleeping when I finally do. I didn't hear you get up."

"Your body's healing," I say. "You need rest."

"So do you," she says, "and you *aren't* sleeping, Shane." Her hand flattens on my chest. "You haven't had more than a few hours of sleep a night in a week that I remember. I know it's been longer."

"I'm fine." I kiss her forehead, and my hands go to her waist. "And you're tiny right now. How much weight have you lost?"

"Enough to pig out on pancakes this morning," she says, her eyes lighting with the idea.

"Pancakes," I repeat, loving the pure joy spreading over her heart-shaped face.

"Yes," she confirms. "Pancakes. With pecans and whipped cream and lots of syrup."

I laugh, which is really a miracle considering all that's happened, but then, she is my miracle. "I can get you pecans, whipped cream, and lots of syrup too. Anything else?"

"Coffee that includes whipped cream and chocolate."

"All right then," I agree. "I'll order room service."

She pushes to her toes and kisses me. "Give me fifteen minutes before you order so I can shower and get downstairs." She twists out of my arms and playfully darts away toward the bathroom, the ease at which she moves telling me her headache really, thankfully, is gone.

She's about to disappear into the bathroom, when my cell phone rings from where I've left it on the nightstand. I grab it and glance at the number, and I am unsurprised that it is once again my mother. I do as I have a half dozen times before: tap the decline button and then stick my phone in my pocket, only to look up and find Emily watching me.

"Your mother again?"

"Yes," I confirm tightly. "My mother again."

"Shane—"

"I'm not talking to my mother before I've had coffee." My gaze slides over Emily's slender body, that pink robe gaping at her breasts, that dark roar inside me looking for an outlet. "Go shower. Before I don't let you." I turn away and head down the stairs, grimacing as my phone rings again in my pocket.

Grabbing it, I decline my mother's call again, and my mind is already elsewhere. I focus on settling down at the stainless steel island in the kitchen, my computer and files in front of me, a cup of coffee in my hand. I pull up my email, fully intending to deal with a few work-related contractual issues, but the top message in my inbox reads: *Funeral arrangements—Derek Brandon.*

My lashes lower, and fuck if my eyes don't burn. My fingers also seem to be tapping the side on the counter of their own accord. I stare at them like they belong to someone else, and then push off the barstool, standing with absolutely no purpose. Out of control. I do not like being out of control. I'm *not* out of control: the company is officially divided, and announcements are set for the week after the funeral, after I tell my father. The offer for the sports complex is in negotiation. Brandon Enterprises will take over the new fashion brand in four weeks. Everything is in order, and yet right now, in this moment, nothing is fucking in order.

My phone vibrates and I grab it, eyeing the text message from my mother: *Why won't you take my calls, Shane?*

"Because I'll have to hear whatever you say all over again when you get here, Mother," I bite out, dismissing her to focus on what's important: Emily.

I tab to my saved numbers and call room service, placing our order. I end the call and set my phone down, pressing my hands to the counter, my chin settling on my chest, that damn email about Derek's funeral grinding along every nerve ending in my body. Emily was right. The funeral is a turning point. It represents everything I can't fix. Everything I can't control. Like the behavior of my damn parents when they return tomorrow night. The funeral isn't closure to me, as Emily suggested, but it is a doorway to a place where I escape what I can't control. And it's on Tuesday. I just need to get past Tuesday.

I push off the counter and sit down, forcing myself to pull up that email again, which turns out to be a bill. I forward it to Jessica to handle and text her a heads-up. Her reply is simply: *Consider it handled.* And it will be. That's one thing about Jessica. She handles things and she doesn't screw around, which I've appreciated more in the past few weeks than ever.

It's also made me appreciate just how important it is that I ensure I really do have control when this funeral is over, which is exactly why I dial Seth. "We need to talk about loose ends," I say, cautious to say nothing that could be recorded and therefore a problem. "Emily's loose ends." Meaning her brother, Rick, and the hacking operation he has her hiding from, with the fear of death if found.

"I expected this call," he says. "And I'm working on options."

"Work fast," I say. "And to be clear: a solution that lacks anything but full closure no longer works for me."

"Also expected, but we need to set a clear, realistic goal. We can't eliminate the threat of the hacking operation. They know her. They see her as a threat."

"All the more reason we can't have Rick running around like a live wire, ready to ignite trouble for Emily. In the time she was in the hospital, there wasn't any ping on his location?"

"Nothing," Seth says. "Which means he's either underground, dead, or a bigger dick than we expected and just doesn't care enough to have shown up."

"That's too many unknowns. I'm done with unknowns. Handle this."

He's silent several beats before he says, "I'll have an update soon."

We disconnect the call, and I sit there a minute, thinking about the irony of her brother being the threat to her safety I fear now, when my brother is dead in a casket after saving her life. After he put her in danger, I remind myself. I can't make the mistake I made with Derek and allow a problem to fester until it becomes lethal. I *won't* let that happen. For now, though, I refocus on my email and move on to business matters, which include an email from the attorney representing the owners of the sports complex, countering my offer by 10 percent. It's expected, which is why I held back 15 percent of the figure I was prepared to offer. I type a reply that makes it seem as if I'll have to work for the extra money, all but done with the deal that will give Martina control over Mike Rogers. There's also an email from Jessica with the contract I've been waiting to proof attached. I pull it up and start reading through the work I masterminded, a document that ensures my father's retirement whether he likes it or not.

Twenty minutes into my review, the doorbell rings and I stand up, heading to the front door to allow room service to set up our covered plates on the island where I've been working. They've just left and I've returned to the kitchen when Emily breezes into the room. "I'm starving!" she exclaims, hurrying toward me, dressed in a pale pink sweat suit. With her cheeks and lips shaded to match, she looks more herself than she has in weeks. "Have you looked under the covers yet?" she asks as I hold the barstool next to mine out for her.

"Not yet," I say. "I didn't want it to get cold."

She lifts the silver tray cover in front of her to stare down at the stack of pancakes drenched in her requested toppings. "They look amazing." She glances over at me. "I'm warning you. I'm going to gain that weight back really fast and will need to eat egg whites while jogging mile after mile."

"I like egg whites."

"For now you get to like pancakes with me. Or . . . what did you get? Please tell me it's not healthy."

"You inspired my hunger," I assure her, lifting my tray to reveal my own stack of chocolate chip pancakes. "I thought we'd share both."

"I love it," she says, and just seeing her love anything makes me love her more. It's crazy, maybe. Or maybe not. But as I watch her now, as I share this moment with her, I fall just a little more in love with her. And I'm going to give her the life she deserves, and won't let anyone, including her brother, take it from her, or us.

I hand her one of the two coffees sitting to my right. "White mocha, with the whipped cream you normally skip."

"I'm really going to start liking all of this stuff too much," she says, sipping her coffee and giving a little moan of pleasure. "I need the doctor to clear me to run again, like, yesterday."

"There's no reason to rush yourself," I say. "You need to go slow."

"But I like our runs," she says. "It's our thing."

"It's one of our *things*," I say, emphasizing the word she'd joked about earlier.

She laughs. "At least we have last night's *thing* back."

I laugh with her and we start eating, talking about our food and landing on the topic of Jessica. "I think there's something between her and Cody."

"There's chemistry there," I say, "but I'd be disappointed if Cody let that happen. Not when he's on our protective detail. He's too close to her."

"And how long do you think we'll need him?"

I set my fork down. "I'm not in a rush to get rid of your protection."

"And there it is," she says, setting her fork down. "The elephant in the room I've avoided. We're still in danger. Martina is still a problem."

"I'm being cautious, sweetheart, and under the circumstances, I think that's reasonable."

"Reasonable because there's still a threat, which I should have already asked about. I've just . . . I've been in denial. Talk to me, please. I thought that once you sold off the pharmaceutical brand, which you've done with Mike Rogers, Martina would be gone."

"It's almost done," I say. "The transition of power is in process. When it's done, he'll be gone, but even then, we'll need to give it time to ensure there are no back doors leading to us."

"Right," she says. "That makes sense. It's logical. We need Cody." She laughs without humor. "I guess the good thing about that is that we force him and Jessica to get to know each other before they clutter it with hot sex."

"Emily—"

"It's okay, Shane," she says. "Really. I'm tough. I think I've proven that."

I draw her hand in mine. "I don't want you to have to be tough."

"Well, I am tough," she says. "And I'm not done with my pancakes." She tugs her hand free. "I think I like yours better than mine."

I hesitate to let her change the topic, but decide it's for the best. I mean, I get it. We all deal with grief and fear differently, and it's not always even what we expected from ourselves. "I happen to like yours better," I tell her, reaching for the plates and switching their locations, setting mine in front of her and hers in front of me. "Problem solved."

"Perfect," she says, grabbing her fork. "I think we both need a nap after this."

"We just got up."

"And your point is what?"

My cell phone rings, and I dig it from my pocket where I'd stuffed it during the room service delivery, note my mother's number, and set it on the table. Emily sets her fork down again. "Is that your mother or your father this time?"

"My mother," I say. "My father stopped trying to reach me."

"Talk to me if you won't talk to them. Why are you avoiding them?"

"I spoke to them when Derek died. My father told me he was in remission and gets to live, but my brother, who he pushed and pushed over the edge, is now dead. The irony of that keeps gutting me."

"I know," she says grimly. "But what about your mother? She lost a son. She needs the one she has left."

"I'll see her tomorrow night when she arrives with my father."

Emily twists around in her chair, facing me and snubbing the food she's been excited over. "She needs you, Shane. You know that right?"

"No, I do not."

Emily's phone starts ringing, and she removes it from the pocket of her sweat jacket. "It's her," she says. "I think I should take it in case they have travel changes or your father—"

"Take it," I say, standing up and moving the barstool to press my hands on the table. "But I don't want to talk."

She nods and answers the call. "Maggie," she says. "Yes. No. I'm fine. Shane's not available, but hold on. I need to put the phone on speaker. It bothers me to hold it to my head right now." Emily punches the speaker button and sets the phone down. "Okay," she says. "I'm here. Are you okay?"

"Are *you* okay?" she surprises me by asking her. Emily's eyes meet mine as my mother adds, "You've been through so much."

"I've been through nothing compared to you," Emily says. "You lost a son."

My mother makes a choked sound. "Yes. I did. And it hurts that I am here and not there. I need to be with my boys. Both of them. Why won't Shane talk to me?"

I lower my chin to my chest, cutting my gaze, hating the mixed emotions I'm feeling right now.

"Everyone deals with things in their own way," Emily tells her. "He's just trying to survive this like everyone else."

"He hates me, doesn't he?"

"No," Emily says without hesitation. "But that doesn't mean he's not angry at a lot of things."

"Of course he is. Of course. How can he not be? I, ah . . . don't even know who I am right now. Is he okay?"

"He's strong," Emily says.

"Are you sure you're okay?" Maggie asks. "Because if anything happens to you, I'm pretty sure I'll be burying another son, and someone will have to bury me too." Her voice cracks, and I hate how much I want to speak up and comfort her. She doesn't deserve my comfort. Not when she undermined Derek and tried to steal the company from him and me.

"I'm doing well," Emily says. "How is Brandon Senior?"

"Ready to be home and dreading it too," she says. "It's real when we get there. The funeral—"

"It's handled," Emily says. "Just concentrate on getting here safely."

"We arrive—"

"Tomorrow night," Emily supplies. "We know. We'll be at the airport."

She's silent several beats and then says, "Tell him I love him." She hangs up.

I lift my head and look at Emily. "That call changes nothing because I don't believe she's changed. And seeing them is going to be hell."

She pushes to her feet and slips under my arm to rest against the table in front of me. "No one understands the anger a parent can create in the midst of loss more than me. You know this. I was, and am still, angry at my father for killing himself. I was angry with my mother for selling out to a man like my stepfather.

And I wish I could tell you that seeing them will wipe away what you're feeling. But it won't. You're going to be angry. Other people are going to be angry. At my father's funeral there was a fight. At my mother's funeral there was a fight."

"Physical fights?"

"Yes. Emotions get high and so does the blame game. There's going to be a fight at this one too, be it physical or emotional."

"I'm not going to let that happen."

"You can't stop it from happening," she says. "And if you don't get some rest, you may be the one throwing the punch. We need to bring down your stress level, at least a little." She flattens her hand on my chest. "So I'm going to be the boss right now. For the rest of today and most of tomorrow, we're going to seal ourselves inside the apartment, order room service often, and do what the rest of the world does."

"Which is what?"

"Watch *Game of Thrones*. We tried it a while back. We hated it. We'll try again and push through the tough stuff. We'll just binge like crazy."

"If I do this, if we do this, I'm going to want to keep you naked, and you could overdo it."

"Stuff me with pancakes, and I'll be so full, I'll be forced to let you do all the work. Which will be a sacrifice and all, but I think I can live with it."

I laugh. I don't even know how that's possible after my mother's call, but I do. "I can do the heavy work, sweetheart. No worries there. And so let's eat more pancakes," I say, fully intending to carry her to bed and strip her naked afterward. Just as I fully intend to ask her to marry me. Just not now. I don't want any part of that new chapter in our lives to be tainted with blood and death.

CHAPTER SEVEN

Over the course of the next twenty-four hours, many things happen.

I actually sleep.

I eat more pancakes with Emily.

I make love to Emily.

I fuck Emily.

I also become more determined to fuck everyone who played a role in killing Derek and almost taking Emily from me.

For that reason, Sunday night arrives too soon and yet not soon enough. I'm ready to get the funeral behind us. I'm ready to get a new life and a new chapter started with Emily. And I'm ready to take actions that ensure the outcome of all this is one that I can live with, which will be an outcome no one else involved will welcome, but must endure. Including my parents, namely my father, who will be handed business news tonight that won't please him.

Thirty minutes until my parents' arrival into Denver, with Cody somewhere nearby shadowing us, Emily and I grab coffee at a spot in the private airport where they're landing.

Both of us are in jeans and boots, our first real clothes in two days, and both of us gravitated to all black without conversation in advance. Funeral black, I think, as we walk to the terminal where my parents are arriving in a private jet.

"Pancakes for your thoughts," Emily says, her hand in my jacket pocket instead of her own.

"I really have none right now," I say, stopping in the waiting area, where we sit down next to each other.

"None?"

"No. None. I'm just ready to get it over with."

"The funeral or seeing your parents again?"

"Both," I say, swigging a drink of my coffee, the thick caffeinated beverage not nearly as heavy as the feeling in my chest, and when I would normally keep that to myself, I don't. Not with Emily. "I have this impossible-to-reconcile sense of dreading the next two days and just needing them over."

"I feel that now too," she says. "It's normal I think, but I felt it intensely with my father, like we both do now with Derek. I think the tragic, unexpected death plays a factor. And I don't think I've told you this, but we lied about my father's cause of death, like you were forced to with Derek."

"You didn't tell me that."

"It was probably me being ashamed. A subconscious thing that made me leave it off, maybe, because I have nothing to hide from you, Shane. It's just that I was—I am—ashamed of my father killing himself. And I know you might be ashamed of some of what Derek did. Even how it led us to that restaurant that night, but in the end, he *saved* my life."

"I know he did," I say, "and when he was in the ambulance, there were no regrets. He was worried about you."

"I want to tell your parents what he did for me, Shane, but I think they might hate me anyway."

"There you go, giving my parents too much credit again. They don't care enough to hate you."

"You're wrong. He's their son. And even if that weren't the case, telling them really isn't about them. It's about honoring the sacrifice he made for me. He gave his life for mine, and I know how greedily he behaved. I know how he fought you and got dirty over money and power. But in the end he showed that he wasn't really that person. You said it yourself. That act of saving me saved his soul. He was selfless."

Her words, etched with emotion and spoken from her heart, bleed into mine. I set my coffee on the floor, stand up, and walk to the window, watching as my parents' plane arrives. "He was selfless," I repeat as Emily joins me. "And I didn't save him. But I was close. That's what guts me more than anything. I was so damn close to pulling him out of the gutter he was swimming in with my father."

Emily takes my arm and we face each other. "I said the same of my father. I didn't save him. I didn't see his troubles. I should have known he was in a bad place. That kind of thinking will gut you."

"And yet you blame yourself for Derek's death."

"He physically put himself in front of me, Shane. It's hard not to take the literal out of that. No matter what led up to it, he died saving me."

I have this mental picture of her lying on the hard floor while I tried to stop Derek's bleeding, and I pull her close, my hand at the back of her head, my forehead against hers. "It killed me to see you like that. *Killed* me."

"Shane!"

At the sound of my mother's voice, my spine stiffens and I inhale a heavy breath. Emily's fingers flex on my chest, and I cover them with mine, kissing them before I turn and slide my arm around her waist. I've barely had time to bring my parents into focus, when Emily sucks in air, and I know why. My mother looks like herself in a black, expensive pantsuit, her long, dark hair tied at her nape, but my father is a stranger: his black slacks and black button-down shirt hang on his thin body, but, more drastically, he's bald. It should affect me. It should blast me with the reality of his mortality that hasn't been erased with a remission that may or may not last. But it doesn't.

I am cold where he is concerned.

And I've barely had that thought before my mother has flung herself at me, hugging me, her head on my chest, as she bursts into tears. My father steps behind her, and in another unexpected moment, I find tears in his eyes. Ice slides down my spine, and there is not one bit of empathy in me for them. In fact, what I feel is hate. I hate them both more than I have ever hated them. Actually, I believe this is the first time in my life that I know I hate them. How can I feel anything else when it took my brother's death for them to actually give a damn about him?

"Shane," my mother says, leaning back to look at me. "Shane, I . . ." Her words trail off as she stares up at me, and she must see what I'm feeling because she struggles for what to say. "Shane, I . . ."

"You need to get home," I say. "Emily and I will meet you there." I lift a hand, and one of the security team members we've hired through Nick's company appears. "Your escort."

My father's eyes meet mine, and yes, there are residual tears. Yes, his eyes are bloodshot. But beyond that, I don't know what I see. I don't know this man, and I am now certain that I never did. And I damn sure know that no matter how long he stares at me, he has no idea who I am. Perhaps with that realization, his gaunt face tightens and he turns away to speak to Nick's man. My mother gives me a helpless look, sobs, and does the same. I still feel cold to their emotions. I still feel hate. I reach for Emily's hand and start walking. She falls into step with me, saying nothing. She just holds my hand a little tighter than normal, and while I wouldn't expect that to be the perfect response to what just happened, it is.

Cody joins us as we exit the airport to the parking lot, wordlessly following us until we reach the Bentley, and then he moves to the black sedan one spot over. Once Emily and I are inside the car, I don't immediately start the engine. I just sit there, inhaling her sweet scent and reminding myself of the gift my brother gave me in her. She leans over and kisses my cheek. Again, not what I expect as the perfect response, and yet it is. And so is getting this night over with, which means going to my parents' house, talking about the funeral arrangements, and ending my father's career at Brandon Enterprises.

I start the engine.

We arrive at my parents' house at the same time they arrive in a black sedan driven by Nick's man. Cody pulls to the curb while I follow the sedan through the gates of the property and around to the back door. I park us in the driveway and kill the engine but make no move to get out of the car, deciding now is the time to prepare Emily for what is to come. "I promised Derek I'd save the company before he died. My way. I promised him I'd save it my way."

"You already have," she says. "You've pushed out Mike and Martina. Or you are about to, anyway."

"Which leaves only one poison."

"Your father."

"Yes. My father. He retires willingly or unwillingly." I glance over at her. "I need to know you're on board with that before we walk into the house."

"One hundred percent. Do what you have to do. And I can handle whatever happens in there."

I reach over, cup her face, and kiss her. "Of that," I say, "I have no doubt. Let's get this over with." I release her and exit the car, fully intending to help her out, but Emily doesn't wait on me. She's out in an instant, and the next few minutes are all about just getting inside the damn house, considering my mother thinks she's lost their keys. And because nothing about this hellish night can just end well, chaos ensues, but finally the keys are found. Emily, thankfully, considering my mother is crying again, takes the lead to herd my parents inside the house while I grab their bags and send Nick's man on his way.

Once I've delivered their bags upstairs, I return to my car, grab my briefcase, and then follow the lights and voices where they lead me. Surprised then to find not just my mother and Emily at the table at the far side of the kitchen, but my father as well. In a normal family, sitting around the kitchen table with coffee cups in hand, as they are, and catching up on news after your parents' return from out of the country would seem normal, even cozy. For my family, it's not. It's a façade of closeness that hasn't existed in years, decades, even, if it ever did beyond my childhood fantasies.

"Have a seat, son," my father says. "Emily was just filling us in on the arrangements for Tuesday."

My mother stands. "I'll get you some coffee."

"I'll share Emily's," I say, claiming the seat next to her.

"We were just talking about the eulogy," Emily tells me, her hand settling on my leg. "It's the only thing that isn't set up yet. Your mother was saying that your father—"

"I'm doing it," I say, no give to my voice. "Just me." My gaze meets my father's, but he doesn't challenge me, which is no surprise. Why would he speak on behalf of his son he all but drove into a grave? And while this might be the appropriate time for me to ask for details on his health, I don't care at this point.

"Emily needs to take it easy," I say. "Which means we need to finish up and get her home." I open my briefcase and remove a folder. "I see no reason to do this in private, Father. It affects us all." I open the folder and remove a document I slide across the table to set it in front of him. "I sold the pharmaceutical branch, as well as the trucking division of the company, for a hefty profit. I then used those profits to move us into another industry."

"Who did you sell to?" my father asks.

"Mike Rogers."

My mother sucks in air, as if she's exposed in this moment, when her rolling around in the sheets with my father's friend and our stockholder has long been known. Unlike her, my father's reaction is no reaction. "And the side deal you've been brokering?" he asks, his tone even, almost bored in nature.

"Complete by the end of the week," I say, "and our commission should be paid within two."

"Define the hefty profits you mentioned in relationship to the sale to Mike."

"Page three of the document."

He flips it open and studies the number before looking at me. "It's an acceptable number to get rid of that leech, *if* these new ventures prove to be smart choices."

I reach into my briefcase and remove another folder, setting it next to him. "Details on those ventures are inside, but I'm not going to review them with you tonight." I grab the remaining document in the folder and set it in front of him. "That's your agreement to retire and name me as permanent CEO of the company."

His eyes sharpen, his energy with them. "I'm in remission, son. I have no reason to retire."

"I'm not letting you take this company down the same path it was traveling before. One, I might add, that got your son killed. I expect that to be signed by Wednesday morning when I return to the office, and then we'll announce the sale to Mike." I take Emily's hand and she stands with me. "And right now I'm taking Emily home to rest."

"And if I don't agree to retire?" my father asks.

"Then I hope you have someone to inherit the company, because I'll be heading to New York with Emily and going back to the job I left to save your company. And last I heard, your other son isn't available to take over when you're gone. You have until Wednesday. I'm taking Emily home, at least the place we call home, for a few more days." I lead Emily around the chair and hold on to her hand as we walk through the kitchen, exit the back of the house, and don't stop until we're in the Bentley.

"If he doesn't agree?" Emily asks.

"I promised Derek I'd save the company, which means that if my father doesn't agree, the gloves come off." I start the engine and get us the hell out on the road, cranking up the radio to a country station, trying to clear my head. Thinking about what comes next if my father refuses to sign those papers. That leads me to a replay of those moments with Derek in the ambulance, on my knee, holding his hand:

"Fuck Martina," he whispers, his expression fierce. "Save ... our company."

"We'll save it together when you get well."

"Promise me. Promise ... you will ... save—"

I squeeze his hand. "Derek."

"Promise me, damn it."

"I promise," I say, hating the sense of "the end" he's giving me. His lashes lower and lift. "Teresa ... tell Teresa ... I ... love her."

"You can tell her."

"Tell her, Shane." There's a white line around his lips that seems to thicken. "Please."

"I will," I promise. "I'll tell her."

"One... last thing..."

"Okay," I say, that word "last" grinding through me. "What is it?"

"Tell Pops... tell him... I'll see him in hell, and he... won't be king."

I snap out of the memory and pull the car into our private spot in the Four Seasons residential parking lot, that memory grinding through my mind and body. Derek's many messages that night are coming back to me. My promises are coming back to me. I have to save the company. I have to get my father out of it. I have deliver that message to Teresa, which I have not. And I have to cherish this woman beside me now.

The music on the radio slides into my mind, a Brad Paisley song called "Then." The lyrics are about the first time he met the woman he fell in love with. "The morning I met you," I say, turning to face Emily.

"The coffee shop," she says.

"I didn't know I loved you then," I say, reaching for her, my fingers tangling in her hair as I pull her mouth to mine. "I remembered that morning over and over while you were in a coma. You *are* my whole world. And I cannot lose you."

Her hand comes to my face. "You aren't going to lose me."

And yet some part of me is uncertain. Some part of me feels the need to hold on to her tighter than ever. Like this isn't over yet.

CHAPTER EIGHT

Monday morning, Emily and I decide to get up and go to breakfast to keep our minds off the funeral the next day, and yet despite that goal, we both end up wearing black jeans and black sweaters. All black. Again. Reality is obviously hard to escape, no matter what we do to try to draw outside of the lines of that reality and into a short-lived fantasy world. Bottom line: tomorrow I bury my brother. Tomorrow I say good-bye to someone who, no matter what our disagreements, has always felt a part of who I am. Today there is no gray to hide within. There is no light. There is just . . . black.

"Getting out of the house is good," Emily says as we exit the bedroom, side by side, and walk down the stairs. "It will make us get out from underneath the sludge of emotions consuming us."

"Sludge," I say. "I couldn't have said it better."

"I wish we could run," she says as we reach the foyer. "Running would give me somewhere to put all this negative energy I'm absolutely oozing."

"Oozing?" I laugh, digging my ringing cell phone from my jeans. "You're full of interesting word choices today," I add, glancing at my caller ID.

"I guess it's a good thing I'm not at work today," she says. "No telling what would come out of my mouth."

"Speaking of work," I say, glancing at my caller ID, "it's Jessica." I hit the answer button to immediately hear: "Mike Rogers."

"What about him?"

"I sent you the draft of the public announcement of the sale," she says. "He's called me twice already and he's a real prick today. Can you review it so I can get this man to go away?"

"I'll look now." I end the call and look at Emily. "Mike Rogers is giving Jessica a hard time over the buyout announcement. I need to review it and let Jessica send it to him. Give me five minutes," I add, already crossing the living area toward my office.

"Do you want coffee?" she calls out.

"This won't take that long."

I've just rounded my desk and sat down when Emily appears in the doorway and my phone rings again. I glance at it and up at her. "My mother this time," I tell her, powering up my MacBook. "Based on recent history, the first call of many to follow today."

"I'll call her," Emily offers. "I handle her better than you."

"You do handle her better than me," I agree, pulling up my email and downloading the document Jessica sent me. "You handle my father better than everyone who isn't sleeping with him, and some who are too."

"That was horrible, Shane," she chides, leaning on the door frame.

"But true," I tell her. "And you know it."

"Sadly," she says, "it is. Maybe it won't be anymore. Maybe this loss will change him."

I give a bitter laugh. "There you go assuming my father is human, sweetheart. He's not. The man didn't even repent when he thought he was dying. He's not going to repent when someone else dies instead." And the truth of those words really pisses me off, as does the fact that my phone starts ringing again. "My mother again," I say, glancing at the caller ID.

"I'm calling," Emily says, "and I'll do it elsewhere so you can concentrate." She disappears into the living room, and I start reading the document, making fast work of sending it back to Jessica.

I've just hung up after calling Jessica when my phone rings yet again, this time a call from Martina's investment group about the sports complex. From there, the morning snowballs into one thing after another, and Emily ends up on the couch in the corner of the office, helping me. Mostly, she's playing middle man with me and Jessica as I try to deal with a combination of condolence calls and business I've neglected over the past two weeks.

It's nearly ten when Jessica arrives to deliver documents I've requested, and of course, she's dressed in fucking black. "A triple shot of gasoline and a white mocha," she announces, cups in hand. "Never say I didn't bring you gifts."

"You're a goddess," Emily says, hurrying toward her.

"I am," Jessica agrees, handing Emily the coffees as the doorbell rings. "Which is why that's a selection of finger foods to get you two through the day. I'll take care of it." She disappears into the living room, and Emily rounds my desk.

I face her and accept the cup she offers me. "Breakfast of champions, right?" she says, her smile not quite reaching her eyes, the barely concealed shadows I find there reminding me of her guilt over Derek.

"Not exactly how we planned this morning," I say softly, my hand settling on her hip.

"At least we're busy," she says. "We needed to be busy."

"I can think of better ways to be busy," I say, and suddenly I wonder why I allowed our plan to deal with today to include anything but us naked and in bed. Or on the couch. Or anywhere.

Her palm comes down on my shoulder. "That wouldn't be good."

"Then you must not be thinking what I'm thinking."

"I am," she says. "But alone, we would have fed that sludge."

"You really must not be thinking what I'm thinking."

"I am thinking what you're thinking. And what you're thinking, at least for me, gets a little emotional."

"Maybe I need to spank you every time you get emotional," I suggest, my voice low, suggestive by intent.

"And what happens when *you* get emotional?"

"I spank your pretty pink ass again."

Her cheeks heat and those shadows fade away. "You're being very dirty."

"You like me dirty."

"Yeah," she says, her teeth scraping her bottom lip. "I kind of do." Her cell phone rings, jolting us from the moment. "And there's a dose of reality," she says. "That will be your mother again."

"Again?" I ask, at the inference that a good deal of those calls she's been taking this morning are related to this one. "What's going on with my mother?"

"The list is long." She starts to move away and I catch her hand.

"What list?"

"She's having pictures blown up for the service," Emily says, sipping her coffee. "And she wants a certain cake, because it was Derek's favorite. And the flowers have to be yellow roses. I could go on."

"She decides all of this now?" I ask. "She's known about his death for two weeks."

"It's the last thing she can do for her son."

"But she didn't want to do it until twenty-four hours before the funeral?"

"Shane," she says softly. "You're being too hard on her. That's your way of dealing with this, though, and I get that. But this is her way. In her time. And I doubt that it felt real to her until she got back here." She presses her hand to my face. "She needs to do this and I'm going to help her."

I cover her hand with mine, searching her face and finding more of those shadows in her eyes. "This isn't just about her. What's going on with you?"

"She reminds me of my mother after my father died," she says, no hesitation to her voice. "A little of me after he died too. Guilt is hard to live with, and neither my mother nor I deserved it. I can't imagine what it's like to know you do deserve it. And before you even go there, you don't deserve it."

"But my parents do. You are who I'm worried about right now. You're supposed to rest."

"I'm going to be medically released later this week. I'm fine."

"You don't have to do this to yourself."

"I *want* to do this, Shane."

Her phone starts ringing again, and as much as I want to hold on to her, to spare her more pain, I look into her eyes, and I know this is part of her grieving process. This is what she needs to do, and I make myself let her go, turning to find Jessica entering the room. "I set up food in the fridge and on the island," she says, crossing to sit down in the visitor chair. "I've also had a delivery sent to your parents' house for this evening and tomorrow morning. There's a catering service handling the gathering at their place after the funeral."

Food and funerals do not sit well right about now, and I change the subject. "Did you bring the contracts legal wanted me to review?"

She purses her lips. "Yes. I did. But really, Shane. They can wait. I told them next week."

"They need them now," I say, trying not to think about yellow flowers and cakes. "Thus why I need them now."

"Fine," Jessica says, reaching into her oversized bag to set a folder on the desk. "But after this, you need to just be with Emily. I'll handle Maggie and everything else. That's what I do. I handle things." She glances at Emily, where she sits on the couch, talking away to my mother, I assume, before returning her attention to me. "Be with her." My phone rings and Jessica grabs it before I can get my hand on it. "I'll get it," she says. "Remember. That's what I do. *I handle things.* And well, I might add." She punches the answer button. "This is Jessica. Can I help you?" Her eyes go wide and she covers the receiver. "Mike Rogers."

"And I handle assholes," I murmur, reaching for the phone and taking the call. "What do you need, Mike?"

"We need to talk terms and transition," he announces.

"Terms and transition," I repeat, leaning back in my chair, amused already by the direction this is taking and all too aware that he thinks the timing of the funeral will weaken my negotiation skills. He's wrong. "The terms are contractual and done. And we'll announce the transition Wednesday."

"I'm not happy with the terms overall."

"You signed the contract," I repeat. "And I have to tell you," I add, "I wrote that document myself. You won't be getting out of it."

"My problem is with the hedge fund operation."

"It wasn't a problem. You were staying in until your contract and investments came to conclusion."

"I've changed my mind."

"In other words," I say, "you discovered my father is alive and well and still managing your money."

"I don't trust him."

"Sounds like the personal problem of a man who can't keep it in his pants." I don't give him time to reply. "Believe me, Mike. As much as I want a clean break, I will not allow this deal to tear apart projects that impact other investors. And I won't open myself and our remaining stockholders up to legal action by those investors you end up hurting."

"How about legal action from me? I spoke to my attorney today. I'm pulling out my money."

"If your attorney told you that you could get away with that, he'd be talking to me, not you. You want out. You find me the money to replace your funds from a source I can get on board with. Otherwise, you're making money. You'll keep making money, and when your contract is up, you're free. But hey. If it helps, I'll ask my father, out of the kindness of his heart, to offer up your spot to someone else."

"This isn't over," he growls, and hangs up, and I have no idea why but my gaze lands on an email from my mother and I open it. It's a mistake that has me staring at photos of Derek and me over the years: playing baseball, at a hockey game. Laughing. Enjoying life. Every photo a knife carving out a piece of my heart.

I close my MacBook and shut my eyes, aware immediately after that Jessica is staring at me. I open them again.

"What can I do?" she asks.

"I need a replacement for my father to run the hedge fund division," I say, agreeing with Mike on one thing. "I don't trust my father, and I won't clean up the company to have him destroy it again."

"I thought your father went into remission."

"He's retiring," I say. "And even if he wasn't, I saved that division in the hopes that Derek would eventually come around and take it over. Obviously, he won't be coming around again ever. I need candidates on my desk Wednesday morning. The best, Jessica. Someone who could swim circles around my father, and that won't be easy. Go make it happen."

"I'll find the best," she says. "But I won't promise you I can do that by this Wednesday. Monday."

"Fine. Monday."

The doorbell rings and Jessica stands. "I'll get it on my way out," she says, grabbing her bag where she's set it on the floor and then hurrying away.

Almost instantly, Emily claims the seat Jessica has just abandoned, her eyes searching mine.

"Say what you want to say," I urge her.

"I know I told you I support you pushing your father out last night. And I do. But maybe you should make big decisions like this after the funeral."

"My decision is made."

"You kept the hedge fund division for a reason, Shane."

"And as I said, I kept it for Derek."

"Are you sure it was just for Derek?"

"One hundred percent."

The air shifts, and my gaze lifts to find Seth standing in

the doorway, his version of black—a gray suit; his version of emotional—a hard-set jaw and no visible emotions at all. Emily twists around in her chair and moves to the side of the desk to face him.

"Emily," he greets her.

"Hey, Seth," she says.

And that's the extent of Seth's ability to make small talk, his attention shifting immediately back to me. "Can I speak to you a moment?"

"I can leave," Emily offers.

"I need air," I say, standing. Yellow flowers, childhood pictures, and Mike Rogers are swimming in my mind. "We'll go to the patio."

Seth disappears into the living room, and I walk to Emily, kiss her hard on the lips, and then head for the door. I've stepped into the living room, and I have no idea why, but I pause, then back up to find Emily sitting in my chair, her hand on her face, obviously upset. "Emily," I say softly.

Her hand falls from her face and her eyes meet mine, surprise on her face. "Whatever you think you just saw, you didn't." She stands up. "Go talk to Seth. I'm fine."

"You're not fine," I say, and I am suddenly angry at how true that statement rings. "But I'm going make sure you are. That's a promise." I turn away and walk to the patio, exiting to join Seth, who is standing at the railing, his back to me.

"Tell me you found her brother," I say, stepping to his side, letting the cold steel of the rail touch my palms.

We face each other, each with an elbow on the railing. "He's been off the radar since before we got involved."

"That's not an acceptable answer."

"Rick didn't just work for—and piss off—a small hacking operation. The Geminis are international criminals, feared by many. They don't make mistakes. If he's dead, he won't be found. Ever."

"And those criminals think Emily knows too much. If he's alive, at any time he could lead them right to her. So I repeat: that's an unacceptable answer. Find him. Deal with him. Make this problem go away once and for all."

His eyes narrow at me. "Make this problem go away," he repeats. "That's a vague use of language. I need you to be specific."

"Find him and evaluate him," I say. "Then we'll define the meaning behind the language. Now, Seth. Not later. If Nick's team can't do the job, hire someone who can."

"Nick isn't the problem here. He and I have worked on this together, and we both believe there's only one solution that meets your need for immediacy, and it's not without risks."

"And that is?"

"Kill off Emily. The *real* Emily, and do it in her hometown, inclusive of a funeral. This, we hope, convinces the Geminis she's gone and no longer a threat. And if Rick's alive, it should lure him out of the shadows."

"Do it."

At the sound of Emily's voice, Seth and I turn to find her standing on the patio, her arms folded in front of her chest. "Kill me off," she says. "Get me off their radar so I know they won't come here."

"What are the risks?" I ask, remembering Seth's warning.

"For starters," Seth says, answering me directly. "Emily's stepfather is dead and missing. Emily's brother is simply missing. Both will be suspects, but that said, as of now they both have passports that show they've been out of the country for several months. They have alibis. They'll be low priority."

"But they'll want to talk to them," Emily presses.

"If they do," he says, "we'll make sure they think they do, through our people."

"You used the word 'risk,'" I point out. "If it's that simple, why that word choice?"

"Because the police investigation is the least of our concerns," he replies, looking at Emily. "If your brother responds to your death by returning home, openly or secretly—"

"The Geminis might kill him," she supplies.

"That's correct," Seth replies.

I expect Emily's retreat from the plan with this news, but it doesn't come. Instead she says, "Right now, if my brother *is* alive, he's like Derek. He has one foot in the grave and is ready to take someone else with him. And it might not be me. It could be someone else. It could be one of you, and I can't live with that. Kill me off."

She's saying what I want her to say and what I believe to be the right choice, but her body is stiff, her voice uneven. "We'll talk about it," I say. "We can decide after the funeral."

"I don't want to talk about this," she says. "I want to do it." She looks at Seth. "When can this happen?"

"To ensure it's believable, we need a month of planning."

"Then start planning now," she says, her eyes meeting mine. "This has always been in the back of my mind, Shane. It's clearly in yours, or I wouldn't have walked in on this conversation. We need to do this."

Anger hums around her, but it's not at me or at Seth. I know this because it's a familiar anger, the kind I know so well, I can all but taste it on my lips. It's what I felt when I was trying to save Derek, and it was magnified when he died and I no longer had that option. "Make it happen, Seth," I say without looking at him, my eyes on Emily.

"I'll update you soon," he says, walking toward the door

and exiting, while Emily walks to the rail and presses her hands to the steel. I step to her side, and together we stand there, staring out at the Denver skyline, seconds ticking by, her thoughts seeming to breathe into the wind until finally she says, "I want to save my brother, but I also want to save us *from* my brother." She glances over at me. "You are probably the only person on this planet who could understand that statement."

"Too well," I agree, relieved that she sees her brother as the threat he could well become. "Too *damn well.*"

She inhales and turns back to the skyline, and silence ticks between us for a full minute or more before she asks, "Does it feel different to you, knowing Derek is dead? Do you feel his absence?"

"Yes," I say. "It does and I do."

"Do you think that's because you know he's dead? Or do you think that's because your world shifted in some way when he died?"

I think of the moment the alarms went off in the hospital, and the sense of dread and death that had come over me. "I knew he was dead before they told me. I felt it."

"My brother's not dead," she says. "I still feel him out there."

So do I, I think. And that's the problem. He's out there, and eventually we both know where this is headed. He's going to be a problem I'm going to have to solve. And when it comes down to it, my brother almost buried Emily. I'm not going to let hers finish the job.

CHAPTER NINE

Afternoon is no different from morning. There are calls. There are challenges. There is the dread of night I soon understand. Turns out that the night before a funeral is as close to hell as the day you find out someone dies. It's you being trapped in that sludge, as Emily called it earlier this morning. It's emotions you don't name because you don't want to feel them. Except one you can't escape: guilt. And that guilt is darkness. You feel it approaching. It's suffocating and you can't breathe. Emily and I survive it with a bottle of wine and pizza. When finally we head to bed, I get Emily talking about the fashion label, and her excitement about everything she feels it can be becomes light in that darkness trying to consume us both. At some point, hours later, she falls silent, resting on my chest. Sleeping.

I don't sleep.

I lie awake and listen to Emily breathing, thinking about the eulogy I'll deliver in only a few short hours. I also think of the promises I made Derek, haunted by the one I haven't even tried to fulfill: Teresa. She disappeared almost immediately after his death, and I let it happen. I haven't tried to find her, because the truth is, I despise her connection to the world that killed my brother. But nevertheless, he loved her. And judging her on the way she stayed by his side, she loved him.

I text Seth: *I need to talk to Teresa. Find her and get her to the funeral.*

His reply is simple and without question: *Message received. Will handle.*

By dawn I've dozed off, only to wake up with the brutal memory of being on the floor of the restaurant, Derek and Emily next to me, blood everywhere. I slip out of bed and manage not to wake Emily, finding my way to the closet to pick out a black suit, one I can later burn as far as I'm concerned. I stand there staring at the rack, and I can't seem to force myself to pick one.

Suddenly Emily is in front of me, looking up at me with those gorgeous pale blue eyes of hers, and something snaps between us. We move at the same moment, and I pull her to me, molding her soft curves to every hard part of me, my hand at the back of her head, my mouth slanting over hers. And then I am kissing her, and she is against the wall, the beast that is my anger, guilt, and pain consuming me. I cup her breast and nip her bottom lip.

She moans, and her teeth scrape my lip, that defiant act driving me wilder still. I rip open the front of the pink silk robe and swallow her gasp. Her panties follow, and my fingers are instantly sliding into the slick heat of her sex, stroking her, teasing her, pressing inside her.

"Shane," she pants, pulling on the band of my pajama

bottoms. "You . . . I want—" Her hand closes over my shaft, and I kiss her again, a deep, possessive, hungry kiss, and when I'm done, I'm not done. I'm just getting started.

I maneuver us, lifting her leg, and I press inside her, lifting her completely off the ground, off the wall. Balancing all her weight myself, a frenzied sway and grind of our bodies follows. And it's good. So damn good that I don't want it to end, and yet it does. She shivers and shakes in my arms and pulls me over the edge with her. I don't put her down when it's over. I hold on to her and carry her to the shower with me, and we repeat the act all over again.

An hour later I'm dressed in my inevitable black suit, sitting at the island in the kitchen, coffee and my computer in front of me.

"We have a situation with your parents," Emily says, joining me, her long-sleeved black dress simple and somehow perfect. Her long brown hair is tied back at the nape of her neck.

"Why does this not surprise me?" I ask.

She stops beside me at the end of the island. "Your father's been gone since midnight last night and hasn't returned, and he won't answer your mother's calls. She's devastated and wants us to come over and ride with her to the funeral home."

"Fucking his woman on the side the day his son is buried," I say. "That's priceless. Maybe I've been too hard on my mother after all."

"You have been," Emily says, "and she really needs us right now."

"We'll go," I say, reaching for my phone. "I need to alert Seth and Cody that we're headed downstairs." I punch in a text before pushing to my feet and following Emily to the coat rack, where she reaches for a coat.

"Do I really need this?"

"It's May in Denver. It's windy, not cold unless it's raining or it decides to snow."

"Snow in May," she says. "I'm not in Texas anymore."

It's one of those random conversations people have when they either want to talk about something else and cant figure out a way, or they don't want to talk about something else so they talk abut nothing.

We head to the door, where I intend to open it for Emily, but she grabs my arm. "Don't decide the worst of your father just yet," she says. "Maybe he's not with a woman. Maybe he is just dealing with this his own way and that means he needed some time alone."

"I'm not judging him by a few hours," I say. "I'm judging him by a lifetime of actions."

"I know. I do, but death has not only marked our near future, it's taken his son. No matter how hard a person you are, that has to shake you to the core. These are extraordinary circumstances. Just, please, for me, I'm asking you to wait to pass judgment."

"For you, sweetheart, I will do anything," I say, but as we head to the elevator, I think of how my parents gravitate toward Emily, like her goodness is a magnet to their evil. And evil always tries to destroy good. We step into the parking garage, and Cody is already in his car, next to mine. And, as if emphasizing the point I've just made to Emily, her phone rings as we're settling into the Bentley. "Let me guess," I say. "My mother."

"Actually, no. It's Jessica." She answers and I reach for the gear shift, only to have her close her hand down on mine. "Wait, I'll talk to him," she tells Jessica, ending the call to look at me. "Jessica stopped by the office to take care of a few things before the funeral, and she noticed a light on in my office area. She wasn't sure how you'd react and—"

Adrenaline surges through me, a sense of dread I don't understand. "Just tell me."

"Your father is in his office, working."

I let out a relieved breath, irritated at the lack of control my extreme reaction showed. "I don't even know what to say to that."

"Security says he's been there since about one in the morning. This must be his way of grieving. I'm going to call your mother so she has some peace of mind."

Grieving in his office, I think. My father. That doesn't ring true to me. "More like he's telling me he won't retire," I say. "And trying to pick that funeral-day fight you warned me about." I place the car in gear. "Let's go to the office."

Jessica's waiting on us as we step off the elevator outside Brandon Enterprises. "Still in his office," she says. "But his door is open and he has people calling for him."

"Of course he does," I say, walking past her and heading into the lobby. I don't stop until I'm at my father's door, where I pause in the open archway.

He's behind his desk, wearing a red T-shirt of all things, probably one of the only T-shirts I've seen him wear in a decade, stacks of files to his left, his attention on his computer screen. I know the instant he knows I'm here, his spine straightening a moment before his gaze lifts to mine. "Hello, son," he says, dropping the pen in his hand and leaning back in his seat, his face so damn gaunt, I barely know him as the asshole that is my father.

I walk toward him, closing the space between us, and I don't stop until I'm on the opposite side of his desk, with my hands pressed to the surface. "Why are you here?"

"I'm running my company."

I don't take the bait. Not today. "You do know you have a son to bury today, right?"

"I'm fully aware of what today is, but this company—"

"Not today, Father. Not today."

"I'm not retiring."

"I said, *not today.* Today doesn't get to be about you."

He erupts and stands. "I know it's not about me. This place is about me and my sons. This place was his too."

"And yet you made him feel that it would never be his, just to entertain yourself."

"To make him stronger."

"He's pretty damn strong now, isn't he? Go home to your wife, who thinks you're fucking another woman right now, because that's what you do. Fuck people you shouldn't be fucking." I turn and walk toward the door. "Like you fucked Derek right into his grave."

"I didn't drive him to his death."

"He didn't die in a car accident, Pops. He died with bullets in his chest from a Mexican cartel. He died trying to win a power struggle you created."

His cheeks redden in anger, and something else I cannot name, spiking in his eyes. "You could have just given him the reins."

"And let him end up in jail," I say. "You're right. I could have, but I wanted better for him."

"You mean you wanted to run the company your way."

"He wanted me to run it my way. He made me promise to save it from you. And I'm going to."

"He was weak. I didn't want him to stay that way."

"Weak?" I say, astounded by how much of an ass he really is, when I shouldn't be surprised. I think of the bullets Derek took for Emily and add, "He wasn't weak. And by the way, his last words were a message for you. He said to tell you, 'Fuck you' and he'll see you in hell, where you won't be king. But he won't see you in hell. He's not there, but you will be." I push off the desk and give him my back, walking toward the door.

"Stop, Shane," he orders, but I don't take commands from him and I don't stop, at least not until I have exited the office and my mother steps in front of me.

"I'm sorry," she whispers before stepping around me and entering the office.

"Why are you here?" she demands of my father. I shut my eyes, the quaking of her voice, the pain in her eyes when she'd said "I'm sorry," jabbing unexpectedly at my heart. "Why are you not at home with me?" my mother continues.

"I have work to do," he says.

"I need you. I need you with me."

"Don't get all prickly with me, woman."

"Don't get prickly with you? Our son is dead. He's dead. He's not coming back. I need you, and you're never there for me. Never." Tears vibrate in her voice. "Why do you think I ended up with Mike? Why? Because you are always with some young girl and you are always gone. You left me alone. And now he's gone. Now Derek is gone and I'm really alone."

Her emotions slam into me, and I step to Emily's desk just to the left of the door, my hands coming down on the wooden surface. And suddenly Emily is rushing toward the office. I push off the desk and turn to watch her pull the door shut. "They need privacy," she says, stepping in front of me.

"I hurt for her," I tell her. "I do. I know he's hurt her. I know she wants Derek back, but it doesn't change the actions she took to destroy him and this company."

"I know," she says. "And she can't take those things back.

We can only hope that she will be a different person moving forward, with or without your father. And you have to forgive her and give her a chance to be that person."

"And if I can't?"

"You can. I know you can."

I'm saved from giving her an answer she won't like when the door to my father's office opens again and my mother joins us. "Please take me to the funeral home."

It's the first time in years I've heard my mother use that word: "please." Maybe that should give me hope that she's going to change and be that different person Emily mentioned. But it doesn't. Hope doesn't live here. Death does. And so do my promises to my brother. One of those promises is unfulfilled, and I text Seth to meet me in the parking garage.

A few minutes later, after Emily insists some private conversation with her might help my mother, I seal them into a black sedan with Cody as their driver. Once they're gone, Seth is waiting for me by my Bentley. "Teresa," I say to him. "Tell me you've found her."

"She left town a week ago, and no one has seen her since, her brother included. I stopped by the restaurant."

"Damn it," I murmur, frustrated at myself for allowing this to happen. "Keep trying," I say. "Even if it's after the funeral." I walk to the driver's side of the car. "Be the fixer that you are. I need you to find her."

I climb into the Bentley and grip the steering wheel. "I'll keep my promise, Derek. Somehow, some way, I'll keep my promise."

There is thunder and gusting winds when we arrive at the funeral home, almost as if Derek is making his presence known. Or maybe it's the devil fighting for his soul, but the devil won't win, at least not when it comes to my brother. My father is another story.

Once inside, there are yellow flowers. So many damn yellow flowers, and they make my mother smile before she bursts into tears. From there, it doesn't get better. With Emily and my mother by my side, we deal with the arrangements. At two o'clock it's time for the visitation, and my father, now dressed in a black suit and tie, walks through the door, more of that wind gusting behind him as he enters from outside. Almost as if that devil he knows is stalking him.

He doesn't look at me. He walks straight to my mother, takes her hand, and leads her to another room. Emily and I exchange a curious look, but then we're greeted by the funeral attendant and a long line of visitors. And so we walk into a room with a closed casket, and before I can even recover the reality of my brother lying inside that box of shiny wood, we have visitors entering the room. It's a full fifteen minutes before my parents, hand in hand, join us. I don't read into their unity.

Eric is there too. He speaks to Emily, concern in his eyes, but she doesn't know he was there that night, I realize. Now isn't the time to enlighten her. And even if it was, Seth joins us, gives Eric a warning look, and Eric quickly departs. He needs to depart. He needs to stay away, and we all need to hope Martina stays away from him.

Come three forty-five, we're fifteen minutes from saying good-bye to my brother.

I stand in a private room for family and close friends, just outside the service room, which is filled to the brim with hundreds of people. A preacher asks us to bow our heads. Emily, my mother, and my father are with me, as are Seth and Jessica and a few random people my mother wanted close to her. We form a circle, and the preacher begins his words of comfort.

I hear them, trying to take solace in them, but I am lost in the regret that this service is at a funeral home for Derek. It feels cold. It feels like he's a number. And he will never be just a number. "It's time," the preacher says, and Emily slides her hand into mine.

We're about to step forward when my mother appears in front of me. Emily releases me, stepping away. "I know you're angry at me," my mother says, tears streaming down her cheeks. "I know you feel I failed him, and you're right. And I will suffer for the rest of my life for that mistake. You have no idea how much I'm going to suffer. You have no idea how much I want to turn back time." She runs her hand down my tie. "I just wanted you to know that." She turns away, and my father offers her his arm as they enter the service room.

Emily is immediately in front of me, her hands at my sides, but she says nothing. She just lets me know that she's with me. I lean down and press my lips to her forehead, letting them linger there a few moments. I take Emily's hand in mine, my gaze finding Seth's, hoping for news on Teresa. He gives me a slight shake of his head, and I accept that some promises will have to wait until after today. What matters is I keep them, and as Emily and I walk into the room, a piano playing somewhere nearby, I start to experience that tunnel vision I had in the restaurant. The room shrinks. The sounds are muffled. The casket is closed.

I only have a vague memory of sitting in the front row between my mother and Emily. I know, though, the minute my mother takes my hand, and the minute Emily does the same. Time fades until the moment they call my name: Shane Brandon.

I kiss Emily's hand, and then I do not know what comes over me, but I kiss my mother's as well. It seems to spark something in her, and the minute I stand up, she is in front of me. "I know this isn't the time," she whispers, stepping to me, her hands gripping my sleeves. "But please forgive me. *Forgive me.*" And there is so much guilt and hurt in her eyes, I believe she is suffering. I believe she will suffer for the rest of her life, and as bitter as I am about Derek's death, she is my mother. And what son wants his mother to suffer?

My hands come down on her arms. "There's nothing to forgive," I say. "It's not your fault."

"It is," she says, tears welling in her eyes. "I should have stepped in. I should have. I—"

"Don't do this to yourself. You're human. And he loved you. He doesn't want this for you. I don't want this for you."

She flings her arms around me, and I can hear Emily's sob behind me. I can hear many sobs. I hold my mother for several beats before I kiss her head and help her back to her seat, surprised when my father aids my efforts. More surprised when I find more tears in his eyes. I turn away from him, my attention landing on Emily, tears streaming down her cheeks. I take her hand, kissing it again, thinking about how right having her in my life is. How impossible it would be for her to be here today if not for Derek.

I walk to the podium, and despite every word I plan to say, I'm remembering what Emily said about honoring his sacrifice. I stand there, replaying so much of that night in the restaurant in my mind, and I start to speak.

"This isn't going to be a long speech, because how I honor Derek is not here at this podium, but what I do when I walk away from it. I knew him better than most. I loved him more than most. I understood him like no one else did.

"Derek was ambitious and driven. That is a curse and a gift given to the Brandon children by their father. Derek took that to extremes, I understand. He wanted to live up to our father's expectations, sometimes without even looking at his own. But no matter what his motivation at the time, Derek wanted to be the best at what he did and he was relentless when he went after his goals. He was a son who admired his father and aspired to run the Brandon empire, and I believe he would have done so and done it in a way that exceeded all expectations. But above all these things, to me, he was my brother, and this world will never be the same without him."

It's then that Teresa walks into the room. I watch as Seth leads her to a seat near the back of the room, and in my mind I see my brother in that ambulance, pleading for me to deliver to her his message.

"Here is what you do not know about my brother," I say. "He was in love, and in the last conversation he had with me, he pleaded with me to tell the woman he loved that he loved her. So, Teresa: he loved you. And I thank you for making him feel loved." Teresa sobs with such fierceness that people turn to find her in the crowd. My parents turn to find her, but I know she will be gone before they ever get the chance to speak to her.

My gaze shifts from the woman my brother loved to the woman I love, my eyes meeting Emily's, and I replay her words in the airport in my mind: *That act of saving me saved his soul. He was selfless.*

"I believe Teresa knows Derek loved her. What she doesn't know, and what few others know, is that my brother died a hero. The details aren't important, but in a split-second decision, he took an action that saved the life of the woman I love." I have to shut my eyes, to fight the burn in them and punch back the emotion balled in my throat. I inhale and lift my lashes to continue. "In the ambulance, he had no regrets over that decision. He wanted to know she was alive. He wanted to know she survived. So much so that I do not believe it's a coincidence that at almost the very moment they brought Emily back from a coma, and when she started breathing on her own, he *stopped* breathing. I believe he waited for her to live before he allowed himself to say good-bye. So today I say good-bye, Brother. And thank you for the gift you have given me. I promise you, I will never take it for granted. Your selfless act and your kindness will never be forgotten."

I step away from the podium, and the pain in the room is like a magnet, pulling me to it, and then crushing my chest. Suffocating me with their emotions, and igniting every feeling in me that I've tried to suppress. I did this, is all I can think. I didn't save him. I could have saved him.

Almost instantly, Emily is in front of me, wrapping her arms around me, and as I hold on to her, I promise myself, Derek, and God himself that I will not repeat my mistakes. I will protect her from everyone and anything that tries to take her from me.

CHAPTER TEN

The short ceremony at the cemetery is a disaster, rain pounding down on us all until, finally, the guests disperse, but I'm simply not ready to leave. I need to say good-bye to Derek my way, on my time. My mother seems to feel the same. She isn't ready to leave either, but between Cody and my father, they manage to get her to the car and on her way home. Emily tries to stay by my side, but as she shivers, I walk her to the car and lock her inside with Seth before returning to the burial plot.

And so here I am.

Alone.

In a cemetery.

And while, yes, Emily wanted to stay with me out of love, ultimately I'm the only one foolish enough to invite myself to stand in the center of the storm. It's where I've always lived and where I belong. It was never where Derek belonged.

I inhale an icy breath, the evening cold, the raindrops splattering down onto the umbrella I'm holding and onto the shiny black casket before me. Every thump seeming to echo with Derek's voice, which I will never really hear again. I stand there trying, though. I try to hear his voice in my head. I try to see his face in my mind. But already I cannot. Already he is lost to me, and I need to find him. I don't know how long I stand there, trying and failing to do just that, and rain gathers on the sleeve of my black trench coat, dripping downward onto my fingers, but in my mind's eye, there is blood, not water, dripping from my hands.

I inhale a heavy breath laden with emotion that I've tried to suppress, but I fail miserably. If Emily was still by my side, I have no doubt that she'd tell me not to suppress it at all. She wouldn't understand that I don't have the luxury of pain and grief. Not yet. Not until I fulfill my promises to Derek, and not until I fulfill my promise to myself to make everyone who should pay for this, pay. I inhale and feel a cool calm come over me. Grief and anger will get me nowhere. Focus and control wins. It's time to take action.

Thunder rumbles overhead, and I turn away from the casket, expecting the black sedan waiting on me with Emily in the back, but that is not all I find. A familiar black Escalade idles several feet behind it at the curb. At the sight of Martina's vehicle, my jaw sets hard and I start walking toward it, and him. The doors don't open, making the expectation obvious that I should climb inside, and I try to decide which I like better: me dripping wet and muddy, or him, forced to join me in the middle of the storm if he really wants to talk. I decide I want him and his expensive suit standing in the rain. I stop walking and wait, but not for long.

An umbrella appears outside of the vehicle, popping open before Martina himself follows, his pin-striped blue suit as expensive as his arrogance, even if he doesn't yet know that to be true. I don't walk toward him. I hold my ground and force him to walk to me. And he's smart enough not to create a standoff. He closes the space between us, his expensive Italian shoes sloshing through the muddy grass.

"Why are you here?" I demand when he stops in front of me, as tall as my six-foot-two inches, his dark eyes meeting mine, no doubt seeing the flecks of blue in my irises burning with that hellfire that is both my torment and my fury.

"To offer my condolences."

"To poke the tiger who wants to rip your throat out," I amend.

"I didn't do this."

"Maybe not directly," I say. "But indirectly. You *are* to blame."

"And you're not?"

He's right. I am, but I've received my punishment with the loss of my brother, whereas he remains unscathed.

Seeming to read my thoughts, he adds, "Everyone who ever said yes to Ramon is dead. I made sure of it." He narrows his eyes on me. "I owe you that and more or I wouldn't be here."

"You're right," I say. "You do. And more. Remember that."

"We have business to attend to."

He means the sports center, of course, and I'll get him his sports center because it serves my agenda, but he won't like my end game. My lips curve with that idea, and I say, "I'll be in touch," before turning and starting to walk away. And I don't look back. At least not now, but this isn't over. I am not done with him. In fact, I haven't even gotten started.

I reach the sedan and open the door, sliding inside and closing my umbrella before placing it on the floorboard. "What just happened?" Emily asks.

My gaze meets Seth's in the rearview mirror, understanding between us. Martina wants everything. He'll get nothing.

"Take us to the apartment," I tell him. "I'll need to pick up my car from the funeral home later."

"We'll pick it up for you," Seth says of his team, and when I nod, he starts the engine. I rotate to face Emily, finding her dark hair tousled and damp, her pale blue eyes filled with concern. "Martina offered condolences as an excuse to inquire about business."

She narrows her eyes on me. "What really just happened, Shane?"

"That's exactly what happened."

"And yet there is more."

I don't lie to her and tell her she's wrong, nor do I insult her by playing dumb. "Until he's gone, there is always more. And that's dangerous."

She tilts her head, a flicker of awareness in her eyes, before, without a word, she faces forward, her body language telling me not to touch her and promising there's another storm on its way before this night is over.

Emily and I step into the elevator of our tower at the Four Seasons and she faces forward. We aren't touching, and in my lifetime, I never thought there would be another human being who I needed to touch the way I need to touch Emily right now, who I needed the way I need her. Every part of me wants to grab her and pull her to me and tear down the wall that has suddenly been erected between us, but I have this sense that the moment I touch her, that storm will erupt. And so we stand side by side in silence as floors tick by. And so we step off the car and onto our floor, and start the walk down toward our apartment, a mile apart when we are only inches from touching.

I unlock the door and hold it open. She is quick to enter the foyer and she doesn't stop walking, charging toward the stairs. I lock the door and catch up with her before she takes the first stair, shackling her wrist and turning her toward me.

She whirls around to face me. *"Until he's gone?"* she demands. "I'm no fool. I know what that means. You want to kill him."

"I'm *going* to kill him."

She grabs my tie. "Don't do this, Shane."

"He will never stop coming at us."

"You're going to end up dead and leaving me with another casket to bury, and I can't do that. I won't stay to watch that happen."

I pull her to me, our bodies aligned, my fingers splayed on her lower back. "It's necessary."

Her hands grip my shoulders. "I don't know the man who believes murder is noooooary."

My fingers tangle in her hair, tugging her gaze to mine. "What part of 'he will never stop coming at us' do you not understand?"

"What part of 'you're going to end up dead' do *you* not understand?"

I rotate her and press her against the wall, a sudden, fierce need to have her naked and beneath me burning through me. "I don't want to talk about death anymore. I just need to fuck you right now."

"That will change nothing."

"And yet I still need to fuck you right now." My mouth closes down over hers, my tongue licking against hers, and I can taste her anger when I want to taste her pleasure. I deepen the kiss and she moans, a soft, sexy sound that promises I'm close to tearing down that wall between us.

I pull the skirt of her dress up her hips, bringing it to her waist, my hand finding her panties and ripping them away. "I don't know why you ever bother wearing these," I say in time with her gasp, tossing her panties aside and shrugging out of my jacket before my hands are at her breasts.

She grabs my tie. "This still—"

"Changes nothing," I supply, my hands going to her backside and squeezing. "Maybe now is when I need to spank you again."

"Spank me because I don't agree with you? That won't make me more agreeable."

My cheek slides to hers, my lips near her ear. "Spank you because it's sexy and we both like it. I would never spank you for any reason but pleasure, and you know it."

"You mean you want something explosive to end our conversation," she accuses. "It won't work."

Anger spikes in me, and I pull back to look at her, my hand tangling in her hair again. "I don't need to end the conversation, Emily. I won't run from it any more than I will from him. But do I want to spank you and make you forget everything but me right now? Yes, I do."

"Damn it, Shane. We have to talk about this."

She's breathless with that demand, and I plan to keep her that way. "Make me," I challenge. *"Fuck me."* I give her backside a soft but firm smack.

She gasps, her lashes lowering and then lifting, her fingers curling around my shirt. "Damn you, Shane," she murmurs, and I see the conflict in her eyes, the need to keep talking, the need to stop talking, before she caves to exactly what I hope for: the need to just fuck, and as if confirming that decision, she grabs my tie and pulls me to her. "This changes nothing. Do you understand?"

I lean in to kiss her and she pulls back. "Say you understand."

"Me needing you won't change," I say. "So *yes*. I understand."

"I need you too, but—"

I lean in, slanting my mouth over hers and licking into her mouth, and she is right there with me. In an instant we are crazy, wild kissing while she yanks my tie free, and I unzip the front of her dress to unhook her bra, my hands finding her high, her perfect breasts, her pebbled nipples. Every dark thought and emotion I've lived this day is now on her lips, and hers on mine. My anger. Her anger. My fear. *Her fear.* And that fear in both of us, the fear that is all about death and separation, is what shakes me to the core, but I plan to drive it away. Now. Later. Forever. Starting with no barriers between us, just naked truth.

I tear my mouth from hers and already her fingers are working the buttons of my shirt. Her soft little hands find my skin beneath it and it's threatening my control, when I want this to be about her. About her fear. Her desire. Her escape and that is my escape. And damn, I need that escape.

I turn her to face the wall, dragging her dress and bra off her shoulders before I slowly drag them down every line and curve of her body, and I follow them to the floor. My arms wrap around her hips, and I discard her dress before sitting her down and removing my shirt and throwing it away. And then my hands are on her ankles, traveling a patient path upward until I'm at her hips and that lush, sexy ass of hers, which I fully intend to spank, but not yet. I want her to wonder. I want to her to anticipate. I want her to forget every fear she has and just be here in this moment. I stroke her cheeks, my teeth and lips at her hip, my body shifting to her side. My hand flattening on her belly.

She sways forward, her hands pressing to the wall, my

fingers walking a path to her sex, my finger finding her nub and stroking. She moans, one of those soft, sexy sounds that I swear thickens my cock and soothes some dark part of me at the same time. Her pleasure, her very existence, is a sweetness, a light I find nowhere in this day and, right now, nowhere in my life. I place my back against the wall, my hand on her hip, my mouth on her clit, licking, teasing. She rewards me with soft moans, her fingers moving to my shoulders, her body melting into my touch.

I cup her backside and start stroking it, then patting it low, right over her clit, preparing to spank her. "When you come . . ." I begin.

"Do it," she gasps, her head tilted downward, hair sweeping her face while her fingers tangle in my hair. "Do it, Shane."

No hesitation. None of that fear. Just trust. I realize then that the spanking isn't about a spanking at all. It's about the trust she just gave me. About how much I needed to know that my honesty about Martina hadn't allowed that bastard to strip her trust away.

"Shane," she whispers, desperation in her plea.

I respond by squeezing her backside and licking her clit, swirling it with my tongue. I start patting her backside again, across her sex, and her fingers tug harder on my hair, her body stiffening, and I know how right *there* the moment is. I quicken my pats and then give her a forceful smack of the cheek, the kind that stings in all the right, erotic ways without causing pain, followed by another, and another. Her sex clenches, her body stiffening, and then I stop.

She gasps with the absence of my palm, trembling seconds before her knees buckle. I catch her hips and ease her down on top of me, her hips straddling mine. Our foreheads come together, our breaths mingling, and her hand is on my face. I reach for it, covering it with mine. "I didn't want to fall in love, now or ever," I admit. "But I did, and you can't possibly know what you mean to me now or you would understand that I *have* to protect you."

"And that's what you don't understand, Shane," she says, pulling back to look at me. "I have to protect you and that's what I'm doing." She leans in and brushes her lips over mine before she whispers, "Because I love you that much."

"God, woman," I breathe out, my hand at the back of her head. "What are you doing to me?" I kiss her then, and it's this slow seduction, the caress of tongue against tongue, and then we are touching each other again, softly, gently. Making love. The V of her body presses against the thick ridge of my erection, tormenting me with every slight move we make. "I need to be inside you," I demand, my cheek to her cheek, my lips to her ear.

"Please," she whispers, and we shift our bodies, maneuvering my pants until I am free and pressing into the wet heat of her sex, stretching her, seducing me.

And as much as I want to move, to *fuck*, to *make love*, when finally she has all of me, I just hold her, feel her. We stare at each other, and when I look into this woman's eyes, I don't shield any part of me. I am me. I am just me, and with no one else in this world am I as exposed as I am with her. It's a connection that terrifies me, because losing her would destroy me. My hand goes under her hair to her neck, and I drag her mouth to mine, drinking her in with a long, slow kiss, our bodies beginning to sway. We start slow, kissing, touching, but there is this burn that refuses to simmer. It's fire that demands more fire, and we are suddenly wild all over again. Hungry. In a frenzied rush of swaying and grinding and kisses that needs to be answered. Has to be answered, and too soon, I think, she's on the edge of oblivion and I'm right there with her. We tumble into that pleasure spot, our bodies trembling, quaking, easing into a sated, quiet place where we are holding each other, the wall behind me the only thing keeping us upright.

But reality returns, and I can feel our battle before this escape return with it. Emily's hands press to my shoulders and she leans back to look at me. "This ends now. A new future. A new start."

"That's what I'm doing. Creating a new future. A safe one."

"By going up against a drug cartel? You can't win that war. Even if Adrian is dead, his father lives. His father will come after us. And don't tell me you'll kill him too. There will always be someone after him."

"Adrian is the one focused on us."

"Until you kill him," she says. "Then it's his father. And after his father, someone else. You need a plan to get him out of your business. Don't kill him and piss off his father."

"He's the reason my brother died and the reason you almost died."

"So this is about revenge."

"He's the reason my brother died and the reason you almost died," I repeat.

"Your brother is the reason your brother died. You know this. You've said this to me. This is your grief and anger talking, and that is a dangerous place to be."

"I know what I'm doing."

"Right. And so do I now, I guess." She scrambles off me, grabs her clothes, and runs up the stairs.

I inhale, giving myself and her a moment to come down from the high of sex, grief, and our argument, because the truth of the matter is, I'm not sure what to say to her. I will kill Adrian Martina, and I feel not one bit of remorse or hesitation on the matter. But now I think I was selfish to tell Emily. I should never have put this burden on her, but to take it off now, I'd have to lie, and lies are my parents' life and breath in misery together. I'm not doing that to us.

Pushing to my feet, righting my pants before I grab my clothes, I follow her upstairs. Entering the bedroom, I can hear her in the bathroom, and I walk to the closet, toss my clothes into the hamper, and pull on a T-shirt. Entering the bedroom, Emily's still not here, and I walk to the bathroom, only to have her appear in the doorway, now wearing her sweat suit.

We stare at each other, the air thick with our conflict, that wall back between us. "I know you don't understand . . ." I begin.

"I understand just fine. But know this, Shane. If you kill him. I will leave you."

CHAPTER ELEVEN

Anger comes at me hard and fast, and my hands are on Emily's waist in an instant, my body walking her body into the bathroom, where I lift her and set her on the sink. My hands come down on the counter on either side of her. "That isn't how this works. You don't get to leave when things get tough. You don't get to leave when you're angry or when we disagree. We fight. We disagree. We don't leave."

"This isn't a fight. This is murder, Shane, and it leads to no place good."

"He's a murderer. I'm doing the world a favor."

"Help the police take him down then."

"All that does is get us more attention with the cartel. Adrian needs to die."

"You're in a dangerous place, Shane. You're thinking with your emotions. And that's not you. See past your need for revenge to a real solution. *End it,* Shane, and that doesn't mean ending Adrian Martina."

I inhale and push off the counter, my hand sliding through

my hair, my gaze lifting skyward. Is she right? Am I consumed
by anger and pain to the point that I can't see clearly? Is my version of control actually the definition of being out of control?

"Derek was jealous of you," she says, drawing my gaze.
"And I read once, and it seems true now, that jealousy is a sharp
object that eventually draws blood and leaves a deep wound.
Don't let vengeance become yours. I can't bury you too."

"And yet you would leave me?"

"I will do anything to get you to think about what you're
doing. *Anything.* And if I have to leave you to save you, then
yes. I will."

The doorbell rings, and I ignore it. "If you leave, I'll come
after you, just like I did before. I know you know that."

"Maybe that will give you something other than murder
to think about."

We stare at each other, a challenge between us, the air
charged and damn near combustible. I take a step toward her
as the doorbell rings again. "Damn it," I say, my hands back on
the counter on either side of her.

"You have to get it," she says, her hands on my shoulders.
"Only our security team and your father can even get up here."

"I know," I concede, straightening, my palm settling on her
face. "We will figure this out, but you aren't leaving me. *Say it.*"

"Shane—"

"Say it, damn it, because today isn't the day to tell me
you're leaving me."

"Oh God," she whispers, her hand going to mine at her
face. "You're right. I'm so sorry. I don't want to leave you. I
don't want to lose you. I'm just—"

I kiss her hard and fast, and then promise, "We will figure this out," before releasing her and exiting the bathroom.

I'm downstairs and at the front door in less than a minute,

opening it to find Seth as our visitor. "I know this is a bad night," Seth says. "But this is important."

Considering Seth doesn't take the word "important" lightly, I back up and allow him to enter, shutting us inside. He doesn't wait for me to invite him into the apartment to get to the point. "This is time sensitive," he says. "I know I told you it would take a month to set up the façade of Emily's death, but it turns out Nick had already been getting ready for this option."

"Meaning what?"

"We have a Jane Doe that fits her description sixty miles from her hometown and less than an hour to claim her as Emily."

Footsteps sound, and Seth and I rotate to find Emily at the bottom of the stairs. "Claim her?" she asks. "What does that mean?"

"For starters," Seth says at her arrival, "we'll connect her to you in the law enforcement databases by way of dental records and fingerprints."

"And I just become this dead woman?" Emily asks, hugging herself.

"Essentially, yes," Seth confirms. "And since this woman has been dead for two weeks, right when you lost contact with your brother, we'll hack the bus system and make it look like you returned home in that timeline."

"But this Jane Doe has a real identity," Emily worries. "What about her family?"

"She's actually not a Jane Doe," Seth amends. "She's a hooker with no family, and a history of drug abuse."

"But you said she's a Jane Doe," Emily argues, her fingers wrapping around the banister, and I don't miss the whitening of her knuckles.

"That was the initial hit on the law enforcement paperwork," Seth explains. "Nick's team intercepted it and found out who she really is, but someone else will too, and soon. We need to act now."

"No one cares she's dead?" Emily presses.

"She has no family or personal connections that we've located," Seth says. "Which is why we're moving on this, and quickly. If we're a go on this, we'll connect the dots to you tonight and leak stories to the press about you being found dead. By morning you'll be all over the local news of your hometown."

"And then we hope my brother shows up," she supplies.

"Yes," Seth says. "Then we wait and watch."

"And if he doesn't show up," Emily says, "we assume he's dead or he just doesn't care enough to show up."

"No," I say, quick to note the hurt in her voice that I want to wipe away. "That isn't the case. He's smart. He could well decide not to risk his life by showing up when he thinks that you're already gone."

"Thanks for that," she says, glancing over at me, "but I know who and what he is, just like you did with Derek." She looks at Seth. "If he shows up, then what?"

"We track him," Seth says. "We monitor him. We know where he is from that point forward, and therefore we keep him, and you, safe."

"But he might not show up," she says. "And then we are back to square one."

"No," I say. "Because he and the Geminis won't have a reason to look for you anymore. They'll think you're dead."

"But what about my current name? My brother set that up. I'm still using it."

"He believes you left Denver," I say.

"Correct," Seth inserts. "And to recap what I put in the file I gave you after we fine-tuned the identity he only partially created: we changed your social when I got involved, and rebuilt your file. I used contacts I have in the government who owed me a favor to ensure your payroll records reflect the social we set up. Additionally, we added a middle initial and sold the social he created to a counterfeit operation that has used it now in three states. You're dead to him, Emily."

"Right," she says. "I'm dead. That's kind of surreal."

"And good," I say.

"And good," she repeats. "I know. It's good." She looks between us. "How long do you think it will be before we know if he'll show up?"

"If he's going to show, I think it will be within a small window," Seth says, "but we'll monitor any activity indefinitely."

"Okay" is all she says, turning to me, those shadows I've seen too often recently back in her eyes again. "I'm good with this if you are?"

"I am," I say.

"Okay," she says again. "I'm going to let you finish up the details. I'll be on the patio." She doesn't wait for a reply, and I don't miss the crack in her voice.

"Are we a go?" Seth asks.

"How are we keeping Rick alive?"

"We'll have men on the ground in her hometown in a few hours."

"All right then," I say. "Yes. Go. And update me in a few hours."

He gives a nod and leaves. I lock up, my hand freezing on the knob as I replay my conversation with Emily earlier: *You're thinking with your emotions. And that's not you.*

She's right. It's not me. And yes, killing Adrian will give me a sense of satisfaction, and yes, the world would be safer without him, but will my family be safer? Will Emily be safer? The answer is maybe not. And I can't live with a maybe that could get Emily killed, which means I can't kill Martina. And Emily needs to hear that right now.

I leave the foyer and head to the patio, finding Emily at the railing, the night air cold, the heater off. I flip it on and close the space between us, stepping to her side. "You're worried about your brother," I say, facing her.

"Yes," she says, rotating toward me, her elbow on the railing. "I'm worried about my brother, but at the same time, I'm angry that he's left us with this hammer over our heads that could drop at any time. I want him to stop being a problem. I want him to stay away and yet I want him to be alive. It's really very confusing."

"Love and family rarely connect by way of logic."

"Kind of like the need for vengeance in the face of pain?"

"Yes, Exactly. You're right about what you said in the bathroom."

"What does that mean, Shane?"

"Adrian wants to go legit. He wants to be on my level. If I am smart about how I deal with him, and I will be, he won't be a problem."

"But you just said you had to kill him to protect us."

"More like, I prefer to kill him."

"Shane—"

I shackle her waist and pull her to me. "I'm not going to kill him, Emily. I'm going to close the deal for the sports center, seal up his relationship with Mike Rogers, and if all goes as planned, we'll have our end game with him, and your brother, in a week."

"Can it just be over now? It's going to feel like a very long week."

"Yes," I agree, "it is, but when it's over, the past will no longer represent that hammer you mentioned, waiting to fall. The past will be nothing more than the past."

CHAPTER TWELVE

Wednesday morning, the day after I've buried my brother, death isn't done with us.

I wake with Emily snuggled against my side, and a text message from Seth: *Reagan Morgan is dead.* I click the link he's sent me to find an article on Reagan from a local Texas news organization, with a photo of Emily with blonde hair. I read through the detail and discover no real surprises, or mention of suspects—just typical news reporting, though I do find myself staring at the old image of Emily that is not that old at all. Not so long ago, that version of the woman I love aspired to law school and a life in a courtroom, just as not that long ago I had called law my career. The difference though is that I walked away from mine by choice, while hers was stripped away, and today, when she wakes up, it's official: she will never be Reagan again. I'm not sure how anyone faces something like that and doesn't feel the blow, even if it's what they ultimately want.

Beside me, Emily begins to stir, and that moment of

revelation for her is about to arrive. She stretches and rises up on her elbow, blinks at me and exhales. "It's happening, isn't it?"

I sit up and take her with me, both of us leaning against the headboard as I hand her my phone with the news piece on the screen. For a full minute, maybe two, she studies it, and the only comment she has when she's done is a question. "Anything on my Rick?"

"Seth would tell us if there were," I say. My concern is her. "Let's talk about you right now. How do you feel?"

"I don't know," she says, sounding genuinely baffled. "I don't think I feel anything." She glances at the phone again, expanding the photo and holding it up by her face. "This isn't me," she says, pointing at the image before eyeing it again. "You know, I use to wish I could be blonde again. But now I don't."

"Give it some time for all of this to pass," I say. "But be blonde if you want to be blonde. No one will be looking for you anymore."

"That's just it. I don't want to be blonde again. That's Reagan. She was the law student who aspired to win every case she fought in a courtroom. She worried about her brother and loved her single-girl apartment. I'm Emily. I want to start a fashion brand. I still worry about my brother, of course. I can't help that, but I also love *our* apartment. I love us. So I guess, really, as angry as I am at my brother, I owe him some thanks as well."

I pull her close and lay us back down, stroking hair from her eyes. "I have a new appreciation for your brother," I say. "I thought you'd be upset."

"Why would I be upset?"

"You're leaving part of yourself behind."

"My mother and father are gone," she says. "My brother too, in a different way. Everything I love and need is here now."

My phone, still in her hand, chooses that moment to buzz with a text message. "That could be about my brother," she says, bolting upright to check the message herself, followed by a disappointed, "or not." I sit up next to her and she hands me the phone. "Your father's already at work." She glances at the time. "At six in the morning."

"Of course he is," I say dryly. "Today's the day we announce the buyout to Mike. We didn't talk about him being there, but I should have known he wasn't going to miss that. I need to get to work before Mike decides to show up and the two of them bump heads." I throw off the blanket and head to the closet.

"No more black," Emily says, joining me by the drawer. "The healing has to start, and you can't dress for a funeral on a day like today." She studies my selection and reaches for the same gray-and-blue-striped Burberry tie she's chosen for me before. "I love this one on you," she adds. "It says power and finesse to me."

My phone rings from where I've left it on the nightstand. "Apparently everyone is early today," I murmur, exiting the closet to grab my phone. I glance at the number and find Emily anxiously watching me.

"Relax, sweetheart," I say, letting the call end to focus on her. "It's one of the investors in the sports center."

"Right. Sorry. I'm just worried about—"

"Your brother," I supply, remembering how she jolted upright with the text message a few minutes before. "I can see that, but today is *not* the day he dies."

"I hope not," she says firmly, as is she's convincing herself that she means it. "Call the investor back and close that deal. I'll grab what you need and hang it in the bathroom." She disappears into the closet and I stare after her, wishing like hell I could make that end game we're after come right now, today, but realistically, it's going to be at least that week I predicted last night.

Refocusing on my call, I redial the investor and talk out the new sports center offer with him. Ten minutes later I disconnect, only to realize that Emily has yet to emerge from the closet. Walking in that direction, I step through the archway to find her removing a black dress from the rack. "I thought today wasn't a day to wear black?"

"I know, but Reagan died today. And that woman they identified as me. She died two weeks ago, and no one seems to care. So I care."

I close the small space between us and take the black dress from her, hanging it back on the rack and retrieving a pale pink one. And now it's my turn to say, "This one suits you. You said no black today," I remind her. "I say no more death today."

"Unless today really is the day my brother dies."

My hand cups her cheek. "He *isn't* going to die today, sweetheart."

"If only you could promise that."

"I can't promise," I agree, "but we have one hell of a team making sure he doesn't. We have to trust them."

"And so we're back to waiting."

"Not waiting. Acting. We make it happen."

"But we wait to find out if my brother will show up."

"Our team is not waiting. They're looking for him."

"While I wait," she says. "Feeling helpless." She blows out air. "At least I have your father today."

My brow furrows. "Why is that?"

"He's a beast of a distraction considering it's all about him and his wants and needs, both of which are always immediate. He won't give me time to think about anything but his demands."

"Well, buckle up, sweetheart. You'll get your distraction for sure. He's up to something or he wouldn't be at the office already. And while I contained myself yesterday with him because of Derek's funeral, I won't be doing so today."

•   •   •

Thanks to another phone call by the same investor I'd spoken to earlier, it's nearly eight, two hours after my father's arrival at the office, when Emily and I exit the elevator and head to one place: my father's office. For her, it's to claim her desk outside his office. For me, it's to ensure that he doesn't get the chance to cause a problem I don't need on the day we announce the sale to Mike. We enter the alcove that is my father's private lobby, and his closed door is no obstacle to me. I walk straight to the door, and I don't bother to knock. I walk right in.

My father looks up from a file he's studying, an amused smirk on his lips, and tosses his pen down. "Glad you're finally at work, son. I haven't seen a copy of the press release on the sale to Mike, and I've made it clear to Jessica I need to see it before it's distributed."

I shut the door and walk to his desk. "Today's your last day."

His gray eyes sharpen. "I'm in remission." He runs his hand over his bald scalp. "I didn't lose my hair to lose my company. I'm not retiring, and we both know you don't have anyone to take over my role."

"I'm managing the existing projects and hiring an expert hedge funder to take over your role, one who won't land us all in jail."

"No one does what I do as well as I do it. And we both know you don't need a distraction from high-heeled shoes and fancy dresses with the Brandon name on them. That is your plan, right? To turn us into some sort of beauty parlor of products?" I have no intention of being baited, and he must sense that in me, because he doesn't wait for a reply, even spinning it as if I might offer one. "Don't waste your breath defending your choice. I'm not going anywhere."

"And when your cancer comes back? Who will take over for you then?"

"You will, Shane."

"If you stay, I leave. And if I leave, I won't come back."

"But you will. Because you'll inherit it, and it hardly seems logical for you to leave your vision behind and start over when I'm gone. I'm running the hedge fund division. I'll allow you to play with your little fashion fantasies, undisturbed."

"Leave it to your wife, as it should be," I say. "If I inherit it, I'll sell it off."

He laughs. "No, you won't. You're invested in the company now, which, by the way, was my plan all along."

I press my hands to the desk. "I'll get the board to vote you out."

"The deal you're brokering for that sports center was my brainchild. No one is going to vote me out when I just made them a small fortune."

"Let me be clear," I bite out. "I still have full control of this company, and I didn't save this division for you or because I felt it was a solid part of our operations."

"The profits are clear," he says. "It's as solid as it gets."

"It's soiled with dirty money, which you've created. I saved it for Derek, not you. He's gone, and now that I'm past the funeral, I'm clear-minded enough to know that we're better off without it." I push off the desk. "I'm delaying the announcement. You can sign an agreement to buy out this division by Monday at fair market value or I'll sell it to Mike." And because I need my mother to stop playing footsie with Mike Rogers, before I set Mike up with Adrian, I add, "And since you don't seem to care about your wife, I assume he'll have your pet project portion of the company at the office and your woman in his bed."

"Mike won't be fucking my wife again. And you won't be

fucking my company. An announcement of my departure on top of Derek's death will create alarm among the clients, stockholders, and staff, which puts our stability at risk."

"You're worried about stability." I give a humorless laugh. "That's comical. I can handle any alarm created by your departure, I assure you." I turn and walk toward the door.

"You're really a prick off the old block," he says, no doubt looking to hit a nerve, and while he succeeds, I don't react.

"I'll email you the new paperwork," is all I say. I exit the office and shut him inside as Emily steps in front of me.

"Well?" she asks anxiously. "How did it go?"

"You don't work for him anymore. Come with me." I settle my hand at her lower back, guiding her forward, toward the lobby.

"I thought today I was with him?"

"You're not," I say. "And you *will not* ever take his abuse again."

We reach the reception area, greeting Kelly before continuing on down the hallway leading to the alcove where my office and Derek's are located. Once at the end of the walkway, I have the option of going left to my office, where a glance confirms that Jessica is sitting at her desk, but I go right, to Derek's office. Guiding Emily to his closed door, I open it and motion her forward. She hesitates, looking uncomfortable, but she enters the office.

I follow her, shutting us inside, and while I've struggled to recall Derek's face or voice, the faint smell of my brother's cologne is here now. And that scent, his presence even in his death, takes me by surprise and punches me hard in the chest.

"What are we doing, Shane?" Emily asks, her hand on one of the visitor chairs, her long, brown hair a striking contrast to the pale pink of her dress. Her nervous energy is something I want to replace with excitement.

"This is your new office," I tell her.

She blanches. "What? No. I can't take his office."

"You can. You will. You know that Derek wanted me to save the company my way, and my way is with your brain-child, our new fashion brand. There's no better place to make that happen than here, in his presence. I've already signed the paperwork. The deal is done."

"I knew you made the offer," she says. "But it's really, completely done?"

"It is," I confirm. "We just need to make a cautious transition of power and smart financial choices. I'm going to email you some files and the contacts for the acquisition when I get to my office. Talk to the major players. Find the major players you want close to you, but do this your way."

The phone on the desk buzzes. "Shane?"

"Yes, Jessica?" I say.

"I have at least three calls you need to take or make right now," she says.

"I'll be right there," I reply, returning my focus to Emily. "Speaking of Jessica. I need her to stay focused on the big picture until I get past this transition period. Unless you really feel you need her now, I'd like to tell her about the 'Jessica' line of clothing and her stock options a few weeks out."

"Of course," she says, but her arms are still folded in front of her. I snag her waist and walk her to me.

"What's bothering you?"

"His office," she says, her hands settling on my chest. "I feel like he needs to be here, not me, but I know he can't be here."

"You're here to do what he wanted. Save this company from my father, and there is no better place than here, in his office. *Your* office. Be excited, Emily. You have no idea how much I want that for you."

"I am. Very. I'm also nervous. I have never handled a major acquisition like this before."

"I'll help you navigate it," I say, "but at the same time, I want this to be yours. Just like the hedge fund operation was my father's."

"Was? So he's officially retiring?"

"He's officially out, just as the hedge fund operation will be soon. With a new day's clarity, I've decided to dump it. I gave my father until Monday to make an offer or I'll sell it to Mike."

"In other words, it got really dirty in there and you want all ties to your father gone."

"Yes. It got dirty. And yes, I want all ties to him gone. It's all part of that end game, sweetheart. I'm going to work. You need to get to work too."

She smiles. "Yes, boss."

"No. I'm not your boss. This is your baby." My lips curve. "Unless we're naked. Then I'm the boss."

She rewards me with a soft, sexy laugh. "I think I want to be the boss."

"Never happening," I promise, walking to the door, but when my hand touches the knob, that scent of Derek is suddenly stronger again, and his lingering presence has me glancing toward his desk to the empty chair that now leaves part of my life empty as well. And yet, in ways, it's fuller than it has ever been. Inhaling, I exit the office and shut Emily inside, heading toward Jessica's desk.

She's on her feet in an instant; her dress so red, it damn near glows, and she rounds her desk and is on my heels. By the time I'm behind my desk, she's standing in front of me. "You're glowing," I say.

"I just got a facial," she says. "So thank you, because it was really brutal."

"I mean your dress."

"Oh. Right. It's a power statement. You're the new king and I'm the king's gatekeeper. Why is Emily in Derek's office?"

"It's her office now. We've officially bought the fashion brand we were eyeing and she's going to run it. More on that later. Don't ask now."

Unfazed by that order, she simply says, "I'll ask her," and holds up a stack of messages. "The top three are related to the acquisition in progress and need your personal attention. The bottom three are random situations I'm capable of handling, but in each case, the parties involved are misinformed enough to believe that you're better, smarter, and in possession of a bigger set of balls than me."

"Convince them yours are big enough to handle what needs to be handled," I say.

"Will do," she says, setting three of the messages in front of me. "I just needed your thumbs-up, boss. Moving on to the announcement. Do you want to call members of the management before we send out the press release?"

"We're holding on the announcement."

"Which . . . means what exactly? What happened?"

"My father happened. Track down Mike Rogers for me. I need to talk to him. And before you start asking more questions, I'll explain once I've put on the brakes with him."

My phone buzzes and my father's voice comes over the line. "Pick up," he orders.

I motion for Jessica to leave and shut the door before I pick up the receiver. "I'm here."

"There's no need to cancel your announcement," he says. "Consider this an offer."

"At what price?"

"Ten million," he says, "which turns this into profit for the board and I assume is acceptable."

"It is," I confirm. "When I have a formal offer, in writing, that is."

"A letter of intent is in your email, but there are conditions."

"Of course there are," I say dryly.

"I have investors who need to be convinced that I'm alive and well. They need stability, which means I need my office to remain as is. I work here, as usual, and we make no formal announcement."

As much as I want to decline, getting this done sheds liability and expedites pairing Mike with Martina sooner than later. "You show up once a week for appearances," I state. "You can hold meetings here if needed and if scheduled in advance with Jessica. And you pay rent."

"I work here twice a week and I have a conference room assigned to me that doesn't require me coordinating with your bitch of a secretary."

"Agreed," I say. "You get twice a week and the conference room, but you'll sign paperwork that designates you as a tenant, and our liability and involvement in your business at level zero."

"Agreed," he confirms. "Make your announcement and get me your paperwork."

"We don't tell Mike about this new development until after the announcement."

"Agreed," he says again, and hangs up.

I stare at the phone, processing how fast and easy that deal was to make with him. And then I laugh. The man's a master manipulator. This is what he was after and I just gave it to him, which means he's got a big money deal in the works. But what he doesn't seem to understand is that I'm happy to give him his deal. I don't want, or need, his dirty money.

CHAPTER THIRTEEN

Immediately after my call with my father, I email Emily the files I've promised her and then dial my contact at the fashion brand we've acquired. In a matter of minutes, I've conferenced in Emily, and not long afterward, I hand the communication and the reins over to her. I've barely ended the call when Jessica buzzes in. "A Jordan Miller is on the line," she says. "He claims to be your father's attorney."

"Eager aren't you, Father?" I murmur to myself before responding to Jessica. "Put him through."

An hour later I've disconnected the call after a verbal brawl, and there is no question that only one day after my father buried his son, he's back to his manipulative ways. My mind gravitates to my mother, who was a wreck yesterday and is now alone, perhaps seeking comfort she won't find with my father. And the last thing I need right now, or ever, is her gravitating back to Mike Rogers when Mike is about to be in bed with Adrian Martina.

I reach for my phone and dial my mother, only to have the

call go straight to voicemail. I bypass the message and dial Seth. "Where's my mother right now?"

"I'm at Jessica's desk," he says.

"Come in," I say, standing up and pressing my hands to my desk, waiting for his entry and answer.

"She's not with Mike Rogers, if that's what you think," he says, stepping into my office and shutting the door. "She hasn't left the house since last night." He crosses to stand in front of my desk. "Is there a new concern about Mike I need to be aware of?"

I push off my desk, shoving my jacket aside to rest my hands on my hips. "My father assures me there isn't, but as I near this deal that pairs Mike with Martina, I'm thinking through anything that could go wrong. And as sure as I free us from Martina, my mother could reconnect us."

"It's a reasonable concern," Seth says, crossing his arms in front of his chest. "I'll make sure she's terrified to go near Mike. Just say the word."

"Your way of fixing things should not involve my mother," I say. "I'll handle it."

"All right," he concedes. "Does this mean we're delaying any part of the process with Mike and Martina?"

"No," I say. "It needs to happen and happen now, and I can't talk to her before the deal is done and risk an emotional reaction. I need my mother intercepted if she goes anywhere near Mike from this point forward."

There's a knock on the door. "It's Emily," Jessica says over the intercom.

I glance at Seth. "She's going to want an update. Is there anything I need to know and prepare her for?"

"Nothing," he assures me, and I immediately instruct Jessica, "Tell her to come in."

The door opens almost instantly, and Emily is inside, shutting it and leaning against it. "Is there news?" She looks to Seth. "Is that why you're here?"

"I work here," Seth reminds her. "And everything is as expected. Law enforcement is looking for your brother and stepfather, but the passports placing them out of the country have rendered them low priority, aside from notifying next of kin. We'll give it a few days and then have one of our staff reach out to them as your brother and stepfather."

"Wait a few days," Emily repeats. "Meaning you want to ensure my brother doesn't show up dead."

It's not a question, and Seth doesn't sugarcoat his confirmation. "Your brother, and/or your stepfather," Seth replies. "But don't hold your breath waiting for your brother to show up. If he's alive, and smart, he won't take that risk."

"And we're stuck with the unknown," she says.

"But you're dead to anyone who might come after you," he says. "That's the end game here." He glances at his watch. "I have a meeting. One final note. Don't Google your hometown or anything to do with your old identity. We're dealing with hackers who can track things in ways you and I can't fathom." He doesn't wait for our confirmation. "I'll keep you updated." He heads for the door and the intercom buzzes. "There's a Becky Newman on the line for Emily."

Emily eyes light up. "Tell her I'll be right there," she says, the worry of moments before banked, at least for now. "She's done work for Louis Vuitton, Shane. I really want her for our team." She turns and follows Seth out of the office, shutting the door behind her. She's distracted now, and that's her sanity. The end game will be mine. I pick up the phone and dial Mike, ready to get that announcement underway.

· · ·

By late afternoon it's done. Mike not only owns the pharmaceutical branch, the news has gone wide, and questions and random challenges erupt. Ultimately, though, the storm passes internally, and the media is far more interested in Mike's status as the owner of a pharmaceutical company and professional basketball team than they are in us. By nine P.M., I'm confident that we've assured tomorrow will be calmer, and I send Jessica home.

Ready to get Emily out of here and home as well, I head for the open door of her office, where I find her standing at the floor-to-ceiling windows framing the room, her back to me. Her floral scent teases my nostrils, mingling with the lingering, barely there spice of my brother's cologne, which proves to be a bittersweet mix of past and present, lost and found. Much like what Emily must feel about a past she's leaving behind for a future she didn't choose but now embraces. Understanding this all too well, I close the space between us, stepping to her side, but I do not speak, nor does she.

For a full minute we both just stand there, staring at the skyline, lights dotting the inky Colorado night, quiet surrounding us, but I can almost hear her thinking, even before she explodes, facing me. "It's really hard loving and hating him this much."

"Believe me, sweetheart," I say, leaning on the edge of the desk. "I get it."

"I was sad and scared this morning, but now . . . now I'm angry. I want him to be alive just so I can throttle him and scream at him. And I don't know what else. I get that we're convincing the world I'm dead and this is our new beginning, but if we don't find him, I'm not going to be grieving him, Shane. I'm going to still feel like that hammer is waiting to fall, with him holding it. You have to feel the same."

"I do," I admit, "but what we're doing right now makes me feel a hell of a lot more secure than I did previously." I snag her hips and walk her to me. "We may never find him, which means we are both going to have to set a deadline to shut this off and mentally declare him dead."

"You're a control freak, Shane. How can you accept this as our solution?"

"By finding a way to control what I can't control. In your brother's case, by paying and trusting the right people, like Seth and his team, to know when, and if, your brother surfaces again. And in your case, I'll buy expensive wine and fill your glass as often as needed until you stop thinking so much." I push off the desk. "Grab your purse. There's a wine bar by the apartment that I've been wanting to show you. We're going to drink too much while talking about your new fashion label."

"Sold," she says. "I can grab my purse on the way out. It's at my old desk outside your father's office."

"I'll grab my briefcase and meet you in the lobby," I say, heading back to my office, where I quickly gather my things, and I'm just about to head for the door when Seth calls, and I can almost feel the tension slide down my spine.

"Just a heads-up," he says when I answer. "Your mother's at home, having dinner with a female friend."

Reading between the lines, I ask, "And my father?"

"With his mistress, in your building."

"Of course he is," I say. "In fact, some might say he's celebrating the death of his son by being a bigger prick than ever." I don't wait on the reply I don't want and that Seth won't offer. "Tell Cody we're on our way to the garage."

"Done."

I grab my briefcase and cross the room, turning out the light, and without a conscious decision to do so, I end up in the doorway of Derek's—Emily's—now dark office. I step inside, and without bothering to turn on the light, I walk to the desk, open the top left drawer, and my hand goes to the black king chess piece inside. A souvenir Derek had claimed after beating my father for the first, and only, time, at age sixteen. It could have been the moment he rose above my father. Instead I believe it became the moment my father decided he would never let Derek win again.

I pocket the chess piece and walk back to the door, pausing before I exit. "You won," I say, as if he can hear me. "He's going to hell, but you aren't there waiting for him."

I exit the office and pull the door shut, walking down the hallway to find Emily waiting for me in the lobby. "Ready?" I ask.

"I am," she says, holding up a black box I know all too well. "This was on my desk with a card that has your name on it."

I take the box and open the card to read the one word inside: *Checkmate.*

"What is it?" Emily asks, indicating the box.

"An aged bottle of Macallan 'M' Lalique with a collector's decanter," I say. "Worth at least ten grand. My father's trademark way of celebrating a five-million-dollar deal, and his way of telling me that I sold him the hedge fund operation right before he closed one of those deals. In other words, he doesn't have to share the profits."

"Do you care?"

"Not in the slightest, but I'll be happy to take the whiskey." We exit the lobby to the corridor outside the elevators and I punch the elevator button. "We'll drink it to celebrate that he, and his dirty money, have left the company." I pull Emily close and lower my lips to her ear. "When the only thing dirty left around here is you and me when no one is looking."

An hour later we're sitting at a table in the dimly lit wine bar, laughing as we debate the merits of a neon red "power" clothing line. "Maybe for the Fourth of July," I joke.

"Tommy Hilfiger does the red, white, and blue as a trademark," she says, and laughs, sipping her wine. "We could do a neon version." She sets her glass down. "And we're joking now, but Jessica made it look good. She owns it."

"My father called her a bitch today."

"Well, she kind of is," Emily says. "But I love her kind of bitch." Her eyes light up. "Maybe we could have a clothing line called 'Bitch.'"

"That would get some attention."

"Exactly," she says. "It would be trending on social media, and even if we could only sell it online, it would get our brand attention."

"I like it," he says. "You just have to decide what statement the 'Bitch' line makes."

"I think it's Jessica's line. It's about her sass." She sips her wine and studies me a moment. "You know. I was thinking of your mother as inspiration for a 'Maggie' line as well. She's elegant and professional. We might even use her in some ad campaigns."

"Just be cautious," I say. "Keep her, and my father, out of the business side of things."

"Of course," she says. "And since we're talking about Maggie. Have you talked to her today? I called to check on her, but she didn't answer or call me back."

"I tried to call her too," I say. "And got the same, but Seth tells me she has a friend over tonight."

"Hmmmm," she says. "Maybe she's too emotional to talk. Sometimes people just need alone time."

"And yet she's with a friend," I remind her, grabbing a bottle of wine from an ice bucket sitting on the empty chair to my left. I refill her glass.

"Who isn't her son who reminds her of her other son."

"She has no idea what an ally you are," I say, refilling my glass and returning the bottle to the ice, when suddenly a familiar man sits down at the end of the table between us.

And he is not a welcome visitor. "Agent Dennis," I greet him, noting his appearance. "Is two-day stubble and a gray suit, which you may or may not have slept in last night, FBI dress code?"

"FBI?" Emily asks, and I don't miss the way her fingers curl into her palms on the table.

"That's right," Agent Dennis says. "I was around the night you landed in the hospital from the car accident that wasn't a car accident."

"Don't play games with her," I warn. "What do you want?"

"Relax," he says to me. And then to Emily: "Really. You can relax. I'm not here to cause trouble."

"And yet you just made that car accident comment," I say.

"To make a point," he replies. "I kept my mouth shut because I know Nick, and he convinced me you're one of the good guys. And I'm loyal to Nick. Or actually to his sister, who I'm in love with but who hates me, which is a long story I won't tell. Bottom line: I know you're doing business with Martina's consortium." He holds up a hand again. "I know. It's legit. And it is, but he's not."

"*What* do you want, Agent?" I repeat.

He taps the table. "To do you a favor in the hopes that, one day, you might do me one." He doesn't give me time to reject that option. "I know your brother was the reason Martina was involved with your company. And I can see that you're separating yourself from anything that might attract him to you. But a man like him likes to come back for seconds. Maybe not now. Maybe not in a year. But eventually."

"I'm not going to help you take him down," I say, "and neither is Emily. So cut to the chase."

"Emily is a weapon he'll use against you," he says. "But you see, he has an Emily too."

"You mean his sister?" I ask. "Because I'm not convinced he'd put her above business."

"He wouldn't," he says. "But Jennie is another story."

I arch a brow. "Jennie?"

"A good girl who fell in love with him before she knew who and what he is," he explains. "And she paid the price. His enemies came after her. He changed her name and gave her a new start." He reaches into his pocket and sets a letter-sized envelope on the table. "That has everything you need to know to confirm this information, but this needs to stay between the three of us and no one else. Once it gets out, it's no longer the life insurance you want it to be."

I leave the envelope on the table. "How do you know about this woman?"

"How I know about her isn't what's important," he says. "I know about her. And now you know about her. It protects Emily. We have to protect those we love from bastards like Adrian Martina. If you ever need to use that name, you'll be remembering Derek and appreciating how true that is. And I'd appreciate you dropping me a few pebbles on Adrian."

"We have to protect those we love," I repeat, narrowing my eyes at him, his motives suddenly clear to me. "This is personal to you."

"Let's just say that I had a brother once too," he says, grabbing a napkin and curling it in his fist. "Nick can reach me if you want or need a buffer between me and you." He glances at Emily. "Nice to meet you, Emily." He stands up and walks away, my gaze tracking his departure when Emily grabs my arm.

"Shane," she says. "We have a problem."

"I'm sure he's a problem," I say. "If he's right—"

"Shane, he took my napkin. He made a point of taking it. That can't be by accident. He was after my fingerprints, which means he must suspect I'm not who I say I am."

CHAPTER FOURTEEN

A moment after Emily drops that fingerprint bomb, Cody claims the seat Agent Dennis has just vacated. "Before you blast me," he says, holding up his hands stop-sign fashion, "letting Dennis get to you was not my call. Nick didn't allow me to intercept him. He wanted to know what the guy was going to say to you."

"Nick should have given me a heads-up," I say, slipping the envelope Dennis gave me inside my jacket pocket.

"I agree," Cody says. "But he's the boss. What did he want?"

"My fingerprints," Emily says. "He took my napkin." She looks between us. "What if he finds out I'm Reagan, a dead girl in Texas?"

"Then he's shit out of luck," Cody says. "Your prints will pull up as Emily Stevens. Just like the woman in Texas who was identified as Reagan pulls up as Reagan."

"We're certain of this?" Emily presses.

"One hundred percent," Cody assures her. "So if he took

your prints, he took your prints. No harm. No foul." He looks at me. "Nick wants you to call him."

"Tell Nick that Dennis offered us his friendship, took Emily's napkin, and left. There's nothing more to tell. He needs to figure out the who, when, where, and why, not me. I'm enjoying a glass of wine with Emily."

"This is where you want me to leave, correct?" Cody asks.

"This is where I want you to leave," I confirm. "And tell Nick to give me a fucking heads-up next time."

"I'll pass that message along," he assures me, and smartly stands, my gaze tracking him as he walks to the door.

"You didn't tell him about Jennie," Emily says, drawing my attention.

"And I'm not going to either," I say. "I trust Seth. We'll get him the envelope in the morning in a discreet way, when no one is watching or standing over his shoulder, expecting me to call him. We'll let him validate the information."

"How bad is this, Shane?"

"If Dennis is being up-front with us, this is good, not bad."

"Do you trust him?"

"I never trust anyone without a hell of a lot of reason to do so," I say. "Which is why we'll have Seth check him out. And why we'll watch him and deal with him with caution."

"He took my fingerprints," she reminds me.

"Which will get him nowhere," I remind her.

"Why would he do that? What does he know?"

"I have no doubt he wants a way to force me to help him. That doesn't make him one of the bad guys. It makes him good at his job."

"He wants to find a way to force you to help him."

"But he won't, and the bottom line here is that our newfound agent buddy gave us a golden ticket. If Martina comes at us outside the boundaries I've set with him, we have ammunition to shut him down and protect our interests and our safety."

"By threatening Jennie."

"It's a chess game, sweetheart," I say. "And should I have to play with Adrian, I will play and win."

"By putting her in danger."

"If anyone ends up dead, it will be him, not this woman. You have to trust me on this. This woman is our insurance. It's protection and peace of mind. This is all good, sweetheart. Not bad."

"Protection from a drug cartel while I'm hiding from a hacking organization." She downs the rest of her wine. "It's like an alternate universe that would be bad, except for one thing."

"What's that?"

"We wouldn't exist if those other things didn't exist too. And I love us."

"I love us too, sweetheart," I say, tossing money onto the table. "Let's go home. Our home."

"Our home," she says, her voice warming. "I will never get tired of hearing those words."

"Neither will I," I say, rounding the table, offering her my hand, and helping her to her feet, our eyes locked, the connection between us suddenly electric. We don't speak, but in unison, we are both smiling. That is the power of this bond I have with her. We can smile for no reason, in the middle of a storm that has yet to fully pass.

I help her with her jacket, my hand covering her smaller one, this deep, clawing need to protect her overtaking me without warning, followed by a flickering image of my brother's casket that I've managed to suppress all day today, until now.

I combat it by inhaling Emily's sweet floral scent and guiding her outside to begin the short walk to our apartment.

We manage two steps and she sways. "Easy there, sweet-heart," I say, catching her waist and holding her close.

"O . . . kay," she says, her hands settling on my chest. "Too much wine for me. Good thing we only have a block to walk. I think I need protection from the sidewalk."

I laugh, turning us forward and setting us in motion. And I indeed protect her from the sidewalk the way I plan to protect her from everything for the rest of our lives. My brother is gone. And no one, most especially Adrian Martina, will ever, ever take Emily from me.

Once we're home and inside our apartment, I help Emily remove her coat, and then carry her up the stairs to the bedroom "No more wine for me *ever*," she murmurs as I settle her onto the mattress. "My God," she adds, kicking off her shoes. "How did this happen? I was fine at the table." The doorbell rings, and she peeks through her fingers. "If that's Nick, you're going to kill him and I can't stop you right now."

"I'm fairly certain he can take care of himself," I assure her as the doorbell rings again. "Go to sleep," I order, heading for the door.

"Not until I know what happens down there," she calls out, and I smile at her groggy voice, certain she won't make it five more minutes before she's out cold.

I head down the stairs, and I'm a few steps from the door when my cell phone buzzes with a text from Seth telling me he's at the door, which I open. "I heard about Dennis," he says, ironically wearing a gray suit not so unlike Dennis's, with one exception: it's pressed. And while I'd assume this indicates Seth is a man of control while Dennis is not, I get the impression that Dennis wants to be underestimated.

I reach into my pocket and hand Seth the envelope Dennis gave me, and then I turn away, walking down the hallway and cutting across the living room to the bar. I've just poured us each a glass of Scotch when he appears by my side, holding up the envelope. "What am I looking at?"

"Supposedly the love of Adrian Martina's life, who's in hiding from his enemies." I take a drink. "A gift from Dennis that he doesn't want shared with anyone, including Nick."

He gives me a two-second deadpan stare and then slips the envelope into his jacket pocket. "What did Dennis want in exchange?"

"If I use the information, he hopes I'll throw him a pebble about Martina—that's a direct quote. The words 'hope' and 'pebble' were both used. There were no demands, and he claims to understand my pain, so to speak, and wants to help."

"That's because his brother was a DEA agent who disappeared while undercover with Martina. And I checked him out after his hospital visit. By all appearances, he's a good agent and a good man. Potentially, an excellent ally."

"Emily believes he took a sample of her fingerprints. I assume he wants the same ammunition against me that he has against Martina."

"Know who you're dealing with and how to control them," he says. "He'd be foolish if he handled himself any other way. A motto that is far from unfamiliar to me or you, since I use it to protect you and yours. But I'll cover all bases with Dennis." He picks up his glass and downs his Scotch. "On another topic. I managed to review your brother's will. He left everything to Teresa, right down to his underwear, but the legal team can't reach her."

"Can you?"

"Yes."

"Then make sure she gets what my brother intended for her to have."

"Understood," he says, glancing at his watch. "I'll check out the information he gave you and text you within the hour." He starts walking, and I don't linger behind to watch him go. I down my Scotch and follow him, locking up after he exits, and then climb the stairs to the bedroom. I pause in the doorway to find both lamps on and Emily under the covers, on her side, her hand on my pillow. There was a time when I swore I would never share my bed with another woman. And then Emily happened.

I walk to her bedside and turn off her light, then cross to the closet, undress, and pull on a pair of pajama bottoms before climbing into the bed. The instant I'm beside her, Emily snuggles up to me, casting me a groggy look. "Did you kill him?"

"Yes," I say, "but I haven't buried the body yet, so don't go downstairs."

"I'll help you find a good spot tomorrow," she says, resting her head on my shoulder. "After we sleep."

I smile, set my phone on the edge of the nightstand, and flip off the light to allow Emily to rest. And rest she does, her body softening against mine, the wine obviously overcoming her worries. I lie there, my eyes wide open, and inside the silence, with the exception of Emily's soft breathing, I'm back to the reality that I've managed to suppress all day. Derek is still gone and my father is still a bastard. And Rick was not only created in the same bastard mold, he's become the biggest threat to her safety. I decide right then that the assumption that he's not a problem, because he believes she's dead, is not good enough.

Emily shifts beside me and I shift with her, my lashes lowering, and sanity comes as I replay that first day I met her, back at the restaurant, sitting across from her. Intrigued by the secrets I already knew she possessed. I remember leaning in, drawing in that sweet scent that I obsess over now. Staring into her eyes as I asked, "Who burned you, Emily?"

A hint of panic flicked through her eyes and then was quickly banked. "Who says anyone burned me?"

"I see it in your eyes," I'd said.

"Back to my eyes," she said, because it wasn't the first time I'd commented on what I'd seen in her eyes.

"Yes," I confirmed. "Back to your eyes."

"Stop looking," she admonished me.

"I can't," I told her, and I still can't, I think now.

And those two words sizzled between us before she said, "Then stop asking so many questions."

I leaned in close then, my lips a breath from hers, my fingers settling on her jaw. "What if I want to know more about you?" I asked.

"What if I don't want to talk?"

"Are you suggesting I shut up and kiss you?"

My lips curve with that memory, my mind going to the first taste of her. So sweet. So damn sweet. And yet there was always something a little wild about her, the promise of the challenge she has proven to be over and over.

I begin to doze off with that thought, with her in my arms, and at some point I must fall asleep, because I jolt awake with Emily shouting out and bolting upright. I follow her to a sitting position, wrapping my arm around her. "Easy, sweetheart. You had a nightmare."

"Yes," she whispers. "Yes, I did." She scrambles out of bed, her fingers sliding into her brown hair before she slips into her pink silk robe while I shift to sit on the edge of the mattress.

"Do you want to talk about it?"

"No. Yes." She turns to face me. "It was a tornado."

"Have you ever been in a tornado?"

"No. My brother's dead." Her gaze goes to her nightstand and she reaches for her phone.

I'm on my feet, intercepting her in a flat second. "Easy, sweetheart," I say again. "Who are you calling?"

"Seth. I need to confirm what I already know. My brother—"

"It was a nightmare, Emily. And what does any of this have to do with a tornado?"

"It's a death thing. For some reason that's how I see death." She draws in a breath and lets it out. "I had my first tornado nightmare right after my father died and for several months following. They started again right after my mother died. My brother is dead."

"My brother is dead, not yours. And *Reagan* is dead. This isn't about your brother, sweetheart."

"Can you just call Seth, please?"

"Yes. I'll call."

I set her phone on the nightstand and walk around the bed to grab mine, punching in Seth's auto-dial and then placing him on speaker. "I'm with Emily on speaker," I say when he answers and Emily and I meet at the end of the bed.

"Jennie checks out," he says, assuming that's why we're calling. "I just got the final reports I promised in the text message I sent early this morning." The one I fell asleep without looking at, I think. "Additionally," he continues, "Nick insists that Dennis would never put someone else at risk for his own cause."

"What's the word on my brother?" Emily asks.

"Nothing's changed," he confirms. "We'll give him a few more days to make contact with the police himself, and if he doesn't, as discussed, we'll do it for him."

Emily folds her arms in front of herself. "He won't make contact," she says, her voice tight. "He's dead." She looks at me. "I'm going to take a shower." She turns and walks toward the bathroom.

"What am I missing here?" Seth asks.

I exit the bedroom to the hallway and take the call off speaker. "It's just you and me again," I say. "And it's a gut feeling she's dealing with."

"She thinks he's dead."

"Yes. She thinks he's dead."

"That might be for the best," he says, no emotion to his voice.

"That he's dead or that she thinks he's dead?"

"Either," he says. "Both give her closure. And let's face it. A dead, dangerous asshole is a lot less painful than a living, dangerous asshole."

We end the call and I press my hands to the railing, but before I can even process my thoughts, I hear, "He's right."

I turn to find Emily in the doorway, still in her robe. "He's right about what?"

"My dangerous asshole of a brother," she says, resting her shoulder on the door frame. "I know who and what he is. We talked about this last night, and me getting all uptight about it was the catalyst to the nightmare that wasn't really about death despite my insistence that it was. I was just so immersed in it when I woke up and made you call Seth."

"If it wasn't about death, what was it about?"

"I went to a counselor years ago about this, and she said the tornado represents anything I can't control. And of all the things that qualify as of late, ranging from a coma to death to Martina, my brother is number one."

"Which is why your nightmare had you focused on him."

"Exactly, but I've come to know that these nightmares come when I'm ready to fight back. It's almost like I need to see myself as helpless to get pissed off at myself for being helpless."

"You are the last person I would call helpless."

"I was in a coma," she says. "And I stood next to your brother's casket. Both scream helplessness. But you know what? Screw helpless and screw my damn brother. I will not obsess over him. He will not keep us from the good. And that good includes our soon-to-be famous fashion and makeup line, which is why I'm going to shower, dress in something fabulous, but not as fabulous as our new lines will be, and go to work." She turns and disappears into the bathroom, but a beat later she's peeking around the corner, a shy, sexy smile in her eyes and on her lips. "I'll be naked any second now if you want to be naked with me." She disappears again.

I don't need to be tempted twice. I pursue her with one thing in mind: if she's naked and I'm naked, it's definitely all good. Everything, it seems, is as it should be.

CHAPTER FIFTEEN

Thursday proves that good is in the air when Emily and I arrive at work to discover my father is out of the office. Unfortunately, he's also with his mistress, but my mother is not with Mike Rogers. She's at the governor's mansion, where she's been hired to redecorate—which I know from Seth, because she won't take my calls. The sports center deal closes, and Jessica and I complete the contracts, which I deliver to the seller's attorney myself. But the ultimate good of this day: after all this hellish juggling, to have everyone on our side sign off on the new offer for the sports center, a necessary evil to ensure that I don't make the offer and not have the backing, it's paid off. By mid-morning I receive a verbal agreement accepting that offer, allowing the written contracts to be processed, reviewed, and once approved, signed.

On Emily's end, "Brandon Style," as she's decided to call the new division, is well underway, the takeover of the old to establish our new, moving along. By evening we've retreated to our apartment to finish our work, changed into sweats, and claimed the island in the kitchen as our workspace. "Room service or something else?" I ask, powering up my MacBook.

"I feel like I need to eat egg whites," she says, tying her hair at her nape. "I've eaten nothing but junk for days, but I'm still three pounds down. I really want macaroni 'n' cheese."

"Macaroni 'n' cheese? Where did that come from?"

"My mother used to make it all the time," she says. "I have her on my mind."

I set my MacBook aside. "Because Reagan is dead?"

"Yes," she says. "Because Reagan is dead, but remembering my mother isn't a bad thing. I might not have agreed with her ignoring my stepfather's bad behavior, but I loved her."

"Of course you did," I say. "Mac 'n' cheese it is." I dial downstairs and place our order, which includes an extra-large mac 'n' cheese. "Done," I say. "Mac 'n' cheese on its way."

"I can't wait," she says, hesitating a moment. "Has Seth sent you any of the news from Texas? I'm curious about how the media is reporting my death."

"He won't send anything like that to either of us by email," I say. "But I can have him bring by the clippings."

"No. Don't. It's just morbid curiosity. It's really not a big deal." She changes the subject. "I want to talk about Brandon Style."

"All right then," I say. "Let's talk fashion."

From there, we plot world domination over dinner once it arrives, and settle on a key component of our success: the recruitment of a well-known designer whose name will put us on the fashion map. "The one I want will cost us a lot of money," she warns. "Any of the names that get us attention will, though."

"How much?"

"I talked to some industry recruiting experts today," she says, setting a piece of paper in front of me.

I glance at the compensation package and whistle. "That *is* a big number."

"Too big?"

"Only if we fail."

"That's not going to happen," she says instantly, her tone and expression fierce.

"I know," I say, leaning in closer to settle my hand on her cheek, the air instantly charging between us in that now familiar way I used to comically believe I could fuck out of my system.

"How?" she asks, the breathless quality to her voice telling me she feels it too.

"It's in your eyes," I say, recalling our first dinner together, as I did while she slept last night.

Her lips—those sexy, kissable lips—curve. "Back to my eyes," she says, following my lead.

"Yes. Back to your eyes."

"Stop looking."

"Are you suggesting I shut up and kiss you?"

"I don't know," she says now just as she had then. "I haven't interviewed you as you have me. I know nothing about you. I want to know if you—"

I lean in, and then my lips are on her lips, a caress, a tease that is there and gone, and yet I linger there, my breath fanning her lips, promising another touch I both need and want, as I ask, "You want to know if I what?"

Her response is to scoot off her barstool, and even before she can sway in my direction, I pull her to me, between my legs, my hand splaying at the base of her spine. "What do you want, Emily?"

"Everything," she murmurs. "Absolutely everything."

"Are you sure about that?" I challenge, thinking of the

battle we had over Martina, of all the parts of me that will always be my father's son.

"Everything," she repeats, inching back and looking up at me. "Don't promise me all good. Don't tell me only the good. Because that's a lie and I hate lies."

I cup the back of her head. "I will never lie to you," I vow, my tongue licking into her mouth, and I let her taste that everything she wants. The man who would kill Martina if he had the chance. The man who will destroy Mike Rogers and lose absolutely no sleep. The man who would die to protect her. And live for her. It's a kiss that is meant to tell all, be all. A kiss that sears. A kiss that bleeds pain and promise.

Her hands slide under my shirt, her palms soft and cool, and yet still my skin burns with her touch. "Everything," I tell her, dragging my T-shirt over my head.

"Everything," she whispers in return, dragging her T-shirt over her head.

My gaze rakes over the swell of her breasts above the black lace of her bra, and she reaches down and unhooks it, tossing it aside, and immediately after, she is toeing off her shoes and then skimming her pants down. They pool at her feet, followed by the tiny lace that are her panties. She kicks them aside, and I travel the path up her legs to the sexy V of her body, where just a hint of blonde hair there reminds me that with everyone but me she has to hide. Not with me. My gaze lifts to her belly, her slender waist. Her breasts and nipples. And when my eyes meet hers, whatever she sees in mine parts her lips. My cock thickens in reaction, my mind conjuring all the places I want her mouth before this night is over. But what I want most is for her to know that everything means she can do anything with me, be anything with me, and it will be about pleasure, about trust.

I stand, my hands settling at that tiny waist, my lips curving when my touch triggers her shiver. I like that she shivers for me. I lift her, setting her on the barstool, my hands on her knees. "The thing about everything," I say, "is that it means *everything*. It means you're open to me in every way." I inch her legs apart. "Exposed to me." I lean back, my gaze raking over her breasts, her puckered nipples. Her sex. "It means," I say, my eyes lifting to hers, "no inhibitions." I take her hands in mine and press them to her breasts. "Show me," I say.

Her breath trembles from her lips, her hands caressing her breasts beneath my hands, and I move them to frame her waist. I lean in, my cheek next to hers, and my mouth at her ear, "Everything means going further, going darker." I drag my lips across her cheek, her jaw, her lips, before I pull back to watch her touch herself. And she does, caressing her breasts, her nipples. She rolls them in her fingers, her head tilting back slightly, her lashes fluttering, lowering. I lean in, tonguing a stiff peak through her fingers and suckling. Her hand goes to my head, fingers slicing into my hair. I lick and tease and use her fingers and mine to tease her and please her.

My hand slides to the wet heat between her thighs, stroking into her sex. Her hands are instantly on my shoulders, her body arcing forward, even as her hips arch into my touch. I tangle my fingers into her hair now, dragging her mouth to mine. As I kiss her deeply, the taste of her is addictive, a drug I willingly crave. I slip two fingers inside her, and she pants into my mouth. I stroke her, hold her, caressing her to a place where she is trembling in my arms. And there is nothing sweeter than this woman trembling in my arms. She shatters for me, trembling, becoming a quake, until she collapses, melting into me, my name on her lips.

I cradle her body and then scoop her up, carrying her to the stairs, where I start the walk up to our bedroom. Holding every-thing in my arms—and the thing about holding everything in your arms is that you have everything to lose. I know this. Losing my brother makes this painfully evident. It makes the moment I lay her in our bed powerful. Right. It makes every touch, every taste that follows, more intense. It makes the moment I'm inside her, buried deep, too soon, and yet I need it and her.

Hours later, after the storm of passion between us is spent, we lie in bed again, and I listen to her breathing, that dark, possessive need to protect her I'd felt at the restaurant last night back again. Maybe it's the side effect of death, and near death, that is too raw, but it reminds me of a feeling I used to get when I was trying a case and knew something was wrong. I was missing something. What am I missing now?

Morning comes, and with the closure of the week, I plan to mark the final, signed closure of the sports center contract as well. Friday also officially delivers the gift that just keeps giving: my father. He's at the office, it seems, solely for the purpose of expressing his impatience for the sports complex closing, no doubt ready to revel in Mike's defeat and get paid for it. "Why hasn't that broker returned the signed agreement?" he demands, buzzing into my office for the third time this morning with no other greeting.

"He has six signatures to acquire," I say. "And I have far more than that once he returns it."

"I hope like hell you plan to make your part happen this weekend," he grumbles. "Call me when the contract is in."

Three hours later he appears in my office, his scalp still smooth, his blue suit draping his thin body. "Well?"

Jessica appears in the doorway, holding up an envelope. "The executed contract just arrived. It's done."

My father glares at her. "It's not done," he snaps. "Every one of our investors has to review this contract and sign it. Get to work." He charges toward her, and she backs out of the office to let him depart.

A moment later she reappears and walks toward me. "I'm shocked this white dress I'm wearing today isn't splattered with my own blood right about now." She holds up the folder in her hand. "I assume you want to review this before I prep any packages we'll need to courier out tonight?"

"I do," I say, accepting the envelope from her. "There will be a total of twelve signatures. Call them and alert them that this is not only happening, but we need it to happen by Monday morning. Courier them the contracts and include a return envelope that's addressed to my apartment."

"In other words," she says, "it's going to be a late night. Good thing I have absolutely no love life."

I read between Jessica's well-defined lines. "What kind of Band-Aid do you want?"

She doesn't ask what I mean. She simply says, "Chanel."

"Use my card."

"What's my limit?"

"Seven thousand."

"God, I love this family," she says. "Let me know when you're ready for me to start making copies."

She exits the office and shuts the door. I immediately pick up the phone and dial Emily. "The contract is in."

"Yay! Do we drink that expensive whiskey your father gave us tonight?"

"After we execute the reverse signatures."

"And then we drink," she says.

"And then we drink."

"And then we're done with *him*."

"Yes," I confirm. "And then we're done with him."

We disconnect the line and I sit there, processing those words: *And then we're done with* him.

My fingers tap the desk. I should be celebrating those words, but the truth is, I'd still feel better if he were dead. I dial Seth, and a few minutes later we stand at the window, side by side.

"I planned to kill Martina," I confess. "After some time had passed and I'd distanced myself from him."

"Time and space is a necessity," he says, never missing a beat. "And killing him might be too humane anyway."

I arch a brow. "You have my attention."

"My suggestion is a slow, calculated plan over the course of a year to eighteen months that includes bad press that won't go away and gets him and his father the wrong kind of attention. Once his father turns on him, we slowly destroy his financial assets. He'll be broke and broken."

"Broke and broken," I say, my lips curving with the idea. "Make it happen."

Just the idea is a weight off my shoulders. Because when you have everything to lose, you want to make sure that anyone who would—or could—take it away is broke, broken, or dead.

CHAPTER SIXTEEN

The rest of the day and into the evening, Jessica and I work to bring together the signing of the contracts. By the time we call it a night, the documents have been delivered to the sports center investors. Couriers are scheduled to pick up the signed documents, as well as cashier's checks, tomorrow morning, delivering them to me at the hotel. And we all know that by Monday, the deal will be finalized, effectively ensuring that everything Martina wanted from the Brandon family is now with Mike. Even my father is pleased, which I care about for one reason: he can get the fuck out of my face and Jessica's.

Everything feels on track, and come Saturday morning, life is beginning to fall into a sweet spot. The hotel staff is managing the packages I'm expecting, and to fight the cool morning mountain air, Emily and I bundle up in thick hoodies and walk to the coffee shop, fully intending to hurry back. Instead it's warmer than expected, and we walk around the neighborhood, since Emily can't run until next week, talking about my family, her family, work, and even a little play.

We're about an hour into the walk when my father sends me a text: *Is it done?*

I text him back: *You know it won't be done until Monday.*

His reply is: *Make sure it's done.*

I show Emily the exchange and she laughs. "I'm sorry, but he's like a cartoon character sometimes. Remaining on the topic of your parents . . . I tried to call your mother again this morning and she just won't answer. Considering how she likes to be in the middle of everything, I'm concerned."

"Considering Mike Rogers's stuff is still pending and about to close, it's not sitting well with me either."

She stops walking and turns to me. "Should we drive to her house and see her?"

"Maybe. Let me find out where she is right now." I text Seth: *Where is my mother?*

He replies by calling. "Believe it or not, she's at home with your father," he says. "On another subject, let's talk about Emily's brother."

"Hold on. She's with me." I point to a secluded bench, and Emily and I sit down before I place him on speaker.

"No news," Seth tells us. "That's good news. We can make contact with the officials Monday and start bringing this to a close."

"But isn't there an investigation into the woman's death?" Emily asks. "Won't that drag on indefinitely?"

"The coroner's report is going to show a drug overdose," he says. "It should wrap up quickly from there."

"I see," Emily says, her fingers curling into her palms. "I won't ask for more details. I'm sure you found a way to make it reasonable that I would do that. Depression or something. So okay. Moving on. What happens if my real brother shows up?"

"We'll intercept him," he says. "Before the Geminis do the same, but we're not expecting him to show up, Emily."

"What about a funeral?" she asks. "Won't something like a burial have to happen?"

"We'll have your brother, or rather, our man acting as your brother, request a cremation, and the remains will be shipped to his location outside the US."

The minute the call ends, Emily runs her hands down her legs. "Well, there it is. Cremated. And it's over." She stands up and I join her as she faces me and asks, "Should we go see your mother?"

My hands go to her shoulders. "I can't think of one damn word to say that sounds good in my head right now."

"That was the right thing to say," she says. "Because it's honest and it's real. What did he say about your mother?"

"You don't want to talk about the funeral or your brother or—"

"There's nothing to talk about. It's strange to think that some woman I don't know is being cremated in my place. But it's almost done, and done is good. What did Seth say about your mother?"

"She's at home with my father, and I'd rather talk to her alone." I glance at my watch. "And I really need to get home and check the status of the contracts. Going with your premise of done and over, I want this done and over."

Once we're home, I grab the packages we've already received from the front desk, and together Emily and I begin making stacks on the dining room table. By late afternoon I have every package expected but one: the one for Adrian's consortium. I dial the manager I've been dealing with, and the call goes to voicemail. I repeat this several times before bed.

I'm up early Sunday morning, skipping a shave and throwing on faded jeans, a Brandon Enterprises black T-shirt that somehow seems appropriate right now, and boots. I leave Emily in the bathroom doing what women do, which is absolutely nothing I understand, except that she smells really damn good after the fact, and make my way to the kitchen. Coffee comes first, then I head to the dining room and sit at the end of the rectangular table to stare at the stacks of contracts, my gaze lingering on the empty spot that should be filled.

My fingers begin to thrum the wooden surface, my mind contemplating all the ways this deal might go wrong. I text Seth the same text message I sent him yesterday: *Where is my mother?*

He answers with: *She just arrived at Sweet Hill Bakery downtown and met an unknown man. When he leaves, we'll follow up and determine who he is. Your father's at his chess club.*

"You're worried."

I glance up to find Emily standing in the doorway, her eyes a striking pale blue that matches the T-shirt she's wearing, her loose-fitting black jeans accenting the fact that I need to feed her this morning. "You're still too thin."

"You're changing the subject," she says. "You're worried about the missing contract."

"Something doesn't feel right. Mike has a lot on the line with his team if the wrong people control the complex."

"And your mother won't return our calls," she supplies.

"It's a concern."

"Seth's people have been watching her, right? Surely they'd know if she was seeing Mike?"

"She's not seeing Mike now," I say. "That doesn't mean that won't change."

"We should go see her, Shane. If she's with your father, so what? Call Seth. Find out where she is right now."

"I know where she's at," I say. "A restaurant a few blocks from here, with a man who isn't Mike."

"As in a date?"

"We don't know who he is, but I wouldn't be surprised. My father was here with his mistress the night before last."

"Oh. Well. That's very disappointing. I don't know why, but I thought, with his cancer and Derek's loss, that they'd find each other again. Why don't they just divorce?"

My cell phone buzzes, and I glance at the text that reads: *He's a banker with USA Bank. Roy Givens is his name.*

"Fuck," I murmur, pushing to my feet, the name Roy Givens brutally familiar. A man who's not only gone to war with my father on various occasions, he's damn near won.

Emily pushes off the wall. "What is it?"

I stand up. "My mother's officially a problem." I hand Emily my phone to read the message, and her eyes go wide.

"If he's involved, he's trying to steal the sports center deal out from under us and screw me and my father. While my mother, I assume, continues to screw Mike Rogers."

"But we have all of the signed agreements except Martina's consortium."

"Maybe Martina decided to cut us out. Same result, but more money for him. We need to go see my mother."

"Yes," she says. "We do. I'll grab my purse."

She darts away, and I text Cody to alert him that we're on our way downstairs. I step into the foyer and shrug into a lightweight black leather jacket as Emily rushes down the stairs, her purse in hand, a knee-length jacket already in place. "I'm ready," she announces.

As am I, I think: to have a little chat with my mother.

• • •

The restaurant is busy when Emily and I arrive, obviously a hotspot for weekend brunch that I've never frequented. Emily and I step through the door and are greeted by the hostess, but we don't need her help to find my mother, who's sitting at a small round table for two, facing us, her companion's back to us. She looks up, her gaze landing on me and her anger is instant, palpable.

"Maybe we should step outside and wait on her," Emily suggests.

My mother leans across the table and speaks to Roy and then stands up. Emily's grip tightens on my arm. "Shane. We should step outside."

"We're staying right here," I say, tracking my mother's path as she weaves through tables, her pantsuit a shade of innocent pink, which is almost comical right about now. *Forgive me*, she'd pleaded at the funeral, in a moment of guilt that wasn't any more honest than she's likely to be right now.

My mother steps in front of me. "Shane," she bites out, my name spoken like a parental scold before she steps around me and heads toward the door, clearly with the same idea as Emily: go outside.

Emily releases my arm, and I pursue my mother out the door, where she smartly walks several feet from the restaurant, away from prying eyes and ears, before whirling on me. "Don't tell me you showing up here was an accident," she says. "We both know it's not."

"Why are you with that man?"

"Why? Why is your father with some twentysomething girl?"

"That's deflection. Why haven't you returned my calls?"

"You turned Mike against me," she accuses, her voice cracking. "You took him from me."

"You were furious when you found out about his plans for

a hostile takeover." I narrow my eyes at her. "Unless that was an act?"

"That's insanity."

"Are you in love with him?"

"I'm in love with your father," she says.

"That's not an answer."

"I *know* you forbid him from seeing me."

"He told you that?"

"Yes," she says, folding her arms in front of her. "He told me that."

I consider the idea that she might really care about Mike, and if I believed that to be true, it would give me at least a short pause in my plans. Except for the fact that Mike walked away from her in a second, and it's interesting to me that she's with yet another man who has a tie to my father. "Why are you with Roy? You know that he's Father's enemy, right?"

"I know that he's not mine."

It hits me then that she wants my father's attention to the point of desperation. "Divorce him."

"He needs me."

"He treats you like crap. And look what you're becoming."

"What I'm becoming is the best me that I've been in years. You don't have to understand that, Son. But you have to accept it."

"That man would destroy Father if he could."

"He thinks he is now, by being with me, which means he's not focused on your sports center deal." With that, she turns and walks to the door.

I tilt my head and watch as she approaches the restaurant at the same moment Emily exits, the two of them pausing to talk, but I'm still focused on the exchange I just had with my mother. Did she just tell me she's distracting Roy because he was targeting the sports center deal that I didn't even know she knew about? And does my father know? Would he endorse my mother sleeping with someone for financial gain? My answer is yes, and it doesn't change my opinion of my father, but my mother proves less the woman I once thought she was every single day.

I set my fucked-up family aside and refocus on the sports center deal. I dial my father. "What does Roy have to do with the stadium deal?"

"He heard rumors about a sale," he says, not even bothering to play dumb.

"And you did what? Distracted him with your wife?"

"Does this call have a purpose?"

"Is someone trying to outbid us on the stadium?"

"It was a rumor we shut down. And you wouldn't be asking this if the contracts weren't signed. What the fuck is going on?"

"The deal will be done Monday," I say, ending the call, my hand settling on my jaw, stubble rasping beneath my palm, a bad feeling sliding down my spine. Why don't I have that signed paperwork? I consider my options and dial Adrian.

He answers on the first ring. "I wondered when you'd call."

That bad feeling officially punches me in the gut. "What's going on, Adrian?"

"We should meet."

"After the paperwork's signed."

"That doesn't work for me," he says, confirming that he's delayed the contract signing.

"This deal is worth a small fortune to you."

"Yes. It is. I have the paperwork with me here at the restaurant. Signed. Come and get it."

"I will not step foot in that restaurant."

"You will if you want this paperwork. And, Shane, bring Agent Dennis with you."

He ends the call.

CHAPTER SEVENTEEN

Aware that I am most likely being watched, I don't give Martina the reaction he might be expecting. I don't panic. I don't rush to act. I slowly lower my phone and consider my options before I dial Martina again. He doesn't answer, which isn't a surprise, but I leave him a message: "If you want to see Agent Dennis, call him yourself. If you want to ask me about Agent Dennis, do it at a time and way that doesn't fuck with my money. I will not be going to the restaurant. I will be going home, where I will first call the investor I had on standby for this deal, and then I will pack to fly out and get the deal done by tomorrow."

I hang up and dial Seth, who answers immediately and listens to my thirty-second rundown of what just happened. "He's baiting you to see how you'll react," Seth says. "Looking for a reaction that tells him you betrayed him. And you won this one. You came at him immediately. You showed no fear. You still aren't showing fear."

"Your assessment of Emily's safety?"

"Going after a man's woman is war. Even the mafia treads on that territory cautiously. But your mother might not be so off-limits. We'll get extra protection on everyone across the board. Kill fifteen minutes there at the restaurant so I can add some layers."

"Understood," I say, breaking the connection and shoving my phone into my jacket pocket.

"Your mother acted very strangely just now," Emily says, stepping in front of me.

"Let's go inside and get coffee and pastries to go," I say. "You need chocolate."

"I do?" Her delicate little brow puckers. "I mean, yes. I always do, but isn't that going to stir the pot with your mother?"

I turn her toward the door at the exact moment the door opens and my mother exits, this time with Roy at her side. Roy is taller than my father by a good foot, a decade younger despite his salt-and-pepper hair, and wears his custom suit far better than my father does right now. And his hand, instead of my father's, is at my mother's spine, directing her toward the sidewalk.

Roy, however, is not overly observant, especially considering he knew I was here. He never looks our way, nor do I sense he knows he's being watched. But my mother does, her chin giving a defiant little lift as they cut right and depart.

"No question they're sleeping together," Emily comments softly.

"According to her," I say, urging us into motion, "Roy got wind of the sports center deal and she's distracting him to buy us time to close it. And my father endorses her doing so."

Emily gives me a disbelieving look. "I can't even find words."

We reach the door and I open it. "It certainly validates my

decision to sell off the hedge fund operation," I say as we enter the restaurant and I scan our surroundings, from the clusters of tables and their occupants to the kitchen door in the far right corner, looking for trouble I don't find.

The hostess eyes us, and I motion toward the glass cases filled with pastries to our left as she greets us. Emily and I step to the register, ordering coffees. "And four of the chocolate croissants," she tells the woman taking our order, indicating them through the glass.

The moment I've paid and the woman departs from the register to fill our order, Emily and I step to the pickup counter, no other customers around us. She turns to me and opens her mouth to speak and then snaps it shut. Her gaze narrows on my face. "What's wrong besides the obvious?"

I'm unreadable to most, a skill that both frustrated and destroyed my legal adversaries, and yet she sees beyond it. My hands come down on her arms. "There's been a development," I say softly.

"With your mother?"

"Beyond my mother," I say. And then, lowering my voice, I quietly and quickly give her the same rundown I gave Seth.

"Okay," she says, remarkably calm considering we're dealing with a man who was there the night she almost died. "This is where I'm going to ask what I asked at the wine bar after Agent Dennis left. How bad is this? Should I be ducking behind a wall instead of standing here, talking to you?"

"If you needed to be ducking behind a wall, I would have already dragged you there and thrown myself on top of you." The words are out before I can stop the memory of Derek that follows. "Martina wants to create a legacy," I say, pushing past my emotional misstep. "He wants to be the Martina that legitimized his namesake, which means this sports center deal."

"You really believe that man wants to go legitimate?"

"I believe he's high on the idea, but not willing to make the sacrifices to remove himself from the crime, or if it would even be allowed by his father if he really tried. Bottom line here: he believes he wants it. I believe that, just as I believe this is a power play. We have to go at him from a position of power."

"You don't think he'll come after me?"

"You are my woman. To hurt you would mean I kill him. That doesn't serve his cause. Now, my mother . . . that could be a different story, which is why I have Seth getting her extra protection."

She blanches and recovers with, "Maybe you should have killed him."

"You don't mean that."

"No," she agrees. "But I wish I did."

"You don't mean that either."

"No," she agrees. "But I wish I did."

"Croissants," the woman behind the counter says, setting a bag down. "Coffee coming in a minute at most."

"I have no idea why I just ordered those," Emily says.

"Because you wanted them," I say. "And inside normalcy is safety. And that doesn't just mean how you feel. It helps us look unaffected by Martina's attempted intimidation."

"Attempted?" she asks. "Did he fail?"

My hand settles at her hip. "Repeat after me. *Yes.*"

"Yes?"

"Coffee," the woman behind the counter announces, setting two cups down.

"Yes," I confirm, going back to our conversation before picking up our coffees and offering Emily one of them. "Try it, like a normal person who loves coffee as much as you do would when they are handed their drink."

She takes a sip. "It's good, and just for the record, we are not even close to being normal people and never will be."

"*That* is true," I agree, my lips curving. "But normalcy is overrated." I hand her the bag of pastries. "Eat these on the walk home. It'll keep your mind off Martina and make us look—"

"As unaffected and normal as the Addams Family? Or the Kardashians? Or—"

I lean in and kiss her. "The Brandons," I say, and the minute I say it, the inference that she will soon share that name electrifies the air between us.

"The Brandons," she whispers.

"Yes, sweetheart," I confirm. "The Brandons." I motion toward the door, my hand at her spine. "Come on."

"Should we tell Seth we're leaving?"

"He knows," I say, scanning the dining area before we head toward the door.

"Maybe I should carry that gun you got me," she says as we step outside. "I haven't touched it since I got out of the hospital." She takes a bite of the croissant. "Oh. Wow. You have to try this. In the name of normalcy and all." She steps in front of me, halting my steps, her hand on my chest, and she holds the croissant to my mouth.

I catch her wrist and take a bite, the sweet buttery flavor touching my lips and tongue, but what I'm thinking about is her, and how, despite her fears, she's managed to be remarkably calm under pressure.

"Well?" she prods.

"Almost as sweet as you."

"We both know I'm *not* sweet."

"On my tongue."

Her cheeks flush. "You're being dirty, Shane Brandon."

"Should I stop?"

"Right now," she says.

I laugh, swoop in for a quick kiss, and then take another bite. "And yes. The croissant is good." I rotate her forward and we start walking again. "We should come back to this place another time."

"I agree," she says. "Even the coffee is good." She glances over at me. "At the expense of really grand small talk about food and coffee, do you really have another investor?"

"I do, but Martina won't let me replace his investment group. I told you. He wants this. We're just playing chess."

We cross the street and approach the hotel. "I'm remembering that day we got home and Martina was waiting at our door, despite all our security."

"That won't happen," I say. "It's what we expect. Which is why he won't do it."

We approach the door and Tai, one of the doormen who is quite fond of Emily, waves in our direction while the double doors slide open to reveal Seth standing just inside the lobby, waiting on us. And since he's smart enough to know that in his perfectly pressed blue suit with his buzz cut and perpetual hard expression that he looks like security, there must be a reason he needs to be in our path. Freeing my hands, I toss my coffee into the trashcan by the door and then drape my arm over Emily's shoulder, keeping her body close to mine. Sheltering her, the way my brother sheltered her.

"Martina's in the bar," Seth announces at the same moment that Cody steps to my right.

"At least this is happening here and now," Emily says, "where we can control the outcome and not wonder what happens next."

Seth arches a brow at her, obviously surprised at her calm

logic, and she follows it up with a glance at me. "How are you going to play this?"

"By ending it," I say. "I need you to go upstairs with Cody." I look at Seth. "This needs to be one-on-one. Me and Martina."

Emily's hand comes down on my arm, but she says nothing more. She and Cody move away, his existence as her bodyguard driving home the fact that our life is not normal, and while I can't change that reality, I intend to make it safer. I refocus on Seth. "Have you alerted Agent Dennis?"

"Nick called him," he says. "And he assured him that he regularly stalks anyone who comes in contact with Martina, and Martina knows this. For him not to visit you would seem strange, and garner attention."

"Stalks?"

"His word," he says. "It's almost like he's trying to get killed. I told Nick to get him fired, hired, or sent to another country on assignment, one that isn't Mexico." He moves on. "Are you armed?"

"No," I say. "But I'll trust you to shoot him if necessary."

He doesn't react, but then, I don't expect him to either. "He's at the edge of the bar by the door, where we have men positioned." He backs up and steps aside, giving me room to depart.

I step forward, my pace even, unhurried, the long shiny white-tiled floor my path. I'm halfway down the walkway when I spy Martina at a sitting area that is basically a square frame with cushions—chosen, no doubt, for the bird's-eye view of the entire bar to his right, and the nearby emergency exit. Essentially allowing him to see anyone who approaches, and react, be it by force or departure or both.

He watches my approach, but my experience in a court-

room tells me that he doesn't do it as a weak attempt at intimidation that I wouldn't feel, but more as a study of his adversary.
Experience also ensures he won't find the answers he's looking
for. I assess him as well, his suit, as always, expensive and pin-
striped, which he seems to favor. He's leaning forward, his
elbows on his knees, and as I near, I can name the brand of
watch on his wrist as a Rolex, while I prefer Cartier. A prefer-
ence that might seem minor to some, most likely to him, but to
me, a Rolex is meant to scream money and power. It's not subtle.
It can scream desperate for power and attention if worn by the
wrong person. And Adrian is desperate for the power and attention he feels his father gets. Which is why he wants this sports
center deal.

I approach the boxed sitting area he occupies, and while
some might feel sitting down with him hands him power, I
don't feel this way at all. I claim a cushion in front of him, my
intent to send him the message that I'm at ease, with nothing
to prove. Comfort and confidence is my power. The sports
center deal is my power.

"I'm surprised you didn't invite yourself on up to my
apartment," I say. "We could have chatted while I packed for
my trip later this evening."

"I was afraid your security team would erupt in seizures,
or I would have."

"The way yours did at the restaurant the night my brother
was murdered and my woman was attacked and nearly killed?"

"Those were not my men, but rather Ramon's."

"They were your men. Ramon simply challenged your
power and won, while my brother lost."

His eyes sharpen, anger crackling off of him. "You test
me, Shane Brandon."

"A test indicates me gauging how future interactions with

you will play out. I have no interest in further interaction with you after today." I lean forward, my elbows on my knees. "When I look at you, I see my dead brother. That's not good for either of us. It reminds me that I want to kill you."

"Is that why you met with Agent Dennis? Because you want me to pay for your brother's death?"

"Agent Dennis wants me to help him put you in prison, but if I do that, and I decide I really want you dead, killing you would get complicated. And I don't like complicated."

His lips quirk, amusement in his eyes. "I'm not easy to kill. In fact, right now, if I snapped my fingers, you'd have a bullet in your head."

"And you'd fall ten seconds later, and you know it."

"We're well matched," he observes, something that might be admiration in his eyes. "And while I knew we had much in common, we are alike in more ways than I ever imagined."

"You see what you want to see."

"I see what you don't want to see," he counters. "And mark my words. One day denial will become cumbersome."

I laugh without humor. "I know I'm my father's son. Do you?"

A muscle in his jaw ticks. "Every moment of every day." He indicates a liquor bottle in front of him. "I owe you a taste of fine tequila." He reaches for the bottle and I wave off the gesture.

"I'll pass," I say. "I have a plane to catch and a deal to ne-gotiate that's larger than some economies."

He reaches into his pocket and tosses an envelope onto the table in between us. "Your cashier's check. The signed contract will be delivered in the next fifteen minutes."

In other words, I was right. He never intended to pull out of the deal. I pick up the envelope and check the contents, confirm the dollar figure, and, knowing anything too easy for this man will be hard for me, I cast him a hard look. "I've moved on," I bluff, setting the envelope on the table for effect. "I'm getting on a plane and signing a new investor tonight."

"And why would you do that, with my money in your hand and me to manage Mike Rogers for you?"

"Define manage," I say.

"He won't so much as blink in your direction when this deal's announced."

I thrum my fingers on the table, seeming to consider the deal, rather than how much I want to kill him. "To be clear," I say. "I'm the broker on this deal and nothing more."

"I'm quite aware of how brokering works."

Ignoring the remark, I continue, "Once I receive your paperwork, I'll send our executed documents to everyone involved, and I'm out. You'll be a weighted stockholder and in charge of setting up your board and operation."

"Excellent," he says. "And then we can get to work on that basketball team we talked about buying or recruiting to our city to compete with Mike's team."

"What part of 'when I look at you, I see my dead brother' do you not understand? I'm done when this is done. You knew that. That hasn't changed."

"We've done well together."

"My brother doesn't agree."

His expression tightens, and he picks up both glasses on the table between us and offers me one of them. "To good-bye."

I accept the glass and say, "To good-bye."

Our eyes lock, and in unison we down the tequila, the liquor sharp as it goes down, nothing compared to what I feel by making a deal with this man. He sets his glass down with a thud and motions to the window. The emergency door opens, but the alarm doesn't go off. "Have a good life, Shane Brandon," he says, standing and walking outside. The door shuts behind him and he's gone. I wait to feel something. Relief. Success. Anything.

I don't. I don't think I'll feel any of those things for a long while. Until the loss of my brother isn't acid burning in a wound.

I pick up the cashier's check and stick it into my pocket, standing as I hear, "Mr. Brandon?"

Turning toward the voice, I find one of the hotel doormen I know in passing standing in front of me. "Yes?"

He indicates a large yellow envelope in his hand. "I was told you should receive this urgently."

I reach into my pocket, remove a bill, and palm it to him before accepting the offering. He walks away and Seth appears in his spot, arching a brow. I open the envelope and find the signed document. "It's done," I say. "And now part two begins. Build him up, make him the stadium king, and then make sure he loses everything. Destroy him. That's what I want you focused on. Which gives you a small window to find Emily's brother, solve the problem that he is, and then focus on Martina."

"By next week—"

"We'll have a Band-Aid. That's not an acceptable answer. I did too little too late to protect Derek. I will not repeat that with Emily. Find Rick, even if you have to dig him up from a hole somewhere." I step around Seth, starting back down that shiny, white tile that might as well be splattered with my brother's blood, the reality of making a deal with the very devil who's responsible for my brother's death a blade jabbing in my heart over and over and over again. The idea that I had to do it because I didn't get rid of him before Derek died adds insult to injury.

That's the thought that carries me to the elevator and all the way to our apartment door, where I pause, Emily's words in my head. *We're not normal.* And while, yes, normal can be overrated, I want her to feel safe. I want her to walk out of our door without a bodyguard and not need to wait on me with one by her side. I want her to know that tonight we're a little closer to that place.

I open the door and enter the apartment, shutting the door behind me. "Shane!" she calls out, exiting the kitchen and hurrying to me, her gaze going to the envelope in my hand. "Is that it? Is it done?"

"It's signed," I confirm, about to explain the details of funding the deal, but I never get the chance. She flings her arms around me, hugs me, and then pushes on her toes to kiss me, whispering, "Checkmate."

I laugh. "Yes, sweetheart. Checkmate." And suddenly, in Emily's relief and excitement, I find the success I denied myself downstairs.

"Now we celebrate," she says, the mischief in her eyes inviting me to places I can't go while Cody lurks somewhere. But his presence doesn't stop me from cupping her head and kissing her, my resolve to protect her never stronger than in this moment.

CHAPTER EIGHTEEN

Ready for the final details to seal the sports center deal, I'm at the office early, making phone calls, while Emily and Jessica arrange the delivery of the executed documents to the entire group of investors. By three o' clock, and just before Emily and I leave for her medical checkup, it's officially done: the deal is not only funded, Brandon Enterprises has been paid and paid well. Between the pharmaceutical and transportation branch sales that we managed to turn a healthy profit on, and the brokered sports center deal, we're sitting on better financials than we were a year ago. And that's not including the hedge fund operation.

Ironically, considering my father's obnoxious need to know everything yet again, he chose today to skip the office job, and in an effort to avoid yet another of his incessant phone calls, I buzz Jessica. "Call my father and tell him we're done."

"As in completely done?"

"Done is done," I say.

"Actually, that's not always true."

I end the connection, my hand going to my silver tie, which I've paired with the gray power suit I bought to celebrate winning my first case, a story I shared with Emily this morning. My lips curve as I remember her excitement that had followed, as well as her insistence, that I wear it for good luck today. I shake my head and wonder how the hell I've gone from a man who wanted women only in bed to smiling at the idea of Emily picking out my clothes? But then, it's rather appropriate, considering she's now running a fashion line. A role it's time to make official in all ways.

With that thought, I stand up and grab my briefcase, as well as the file on my desk that I've been saving for Emily. Crossing my office, I flip out the light, and considering Jessica's recent long hours, I exit my office and say, "Go home," as I walk past her desk.

"We must really be done," she calls after me, and I shake my head at her smartass comment, holding up my arm to point toward the lobby just before I step inside Emily's doorway.

The instant she sees me, she pops to her feet and grabs her purse from her drawer, sliding it over her shoulder and looking every bit the executive she is in a navy-blue dress suit. "I'm ready," she says.

I step inside the room and shut the door. "Let's sit and talk about work for a few minutes first," I say, choosing my words carefully as to not to alarm her over her brother.

"Okay," she says, sinking into her chair, her brow furrowed.

I cross the room, set my briefcase down, and then choose the seat across from her, my intent to give her the position of power that she's earned. The folder in my hand then goes on the desk in front of her. "Look at the numbers inside."

She flips it open and studies it for about sixty seconds before her gaze jerks to mine. "What is this, Shane?"

"A survey of salaries for executives in your role in the fashion and beauty industry, inclusive of experience and time served. As you can see, you're being grossly underpaid for your new role."

She shuts the folder and slides it toward me. "I'm not doing this for money."

"When you planned to go to law school, did you plan to make money?"

"Well, yes. Of course."

"The kind of money that would allow you to buy your own Bentley?"

"Shane—"

"Answer me."

"Yes."

"And you think now, starting a major fashion brand, that your work and efforts mean you should earn less?"

"You're trying to compensate for the loss of my legal career," she says. "You didn't take that from me; my brother did. And, Shane, I love you for this. I do, but no."

"Anticipating that comment is exactly why I had human resources provide that data." I open the folder again and pull out page two, setting it in front of her. "This is your new compensation package, which includes bonuses for profits."

She glances down at it and her eyes go wide. "No."

"Yes. It's done." I stand. "Let's go get you cleared by the doctor."

She doesn't move. "Shane."

I walk around the desk and turn her chair to face me, my hands pressed to the arms. "You earned this. This business endeavor is your brainchild, and it was you who found the acquisition. And now you work to get it off the ground. Stop convincing yourself this is about anything but your success."

She inhales and lets out the breath. "This isn't you trying to make me feel better?"

"This is me feeling lucky as hell I have you running this operation." I help her to her feet, my hands at her waist. "Be happy."

"I am. More than I thought possible a few months ago."

"Then let's go get your medical clearance and go home and celebrate."

An hour later I sit in the lobby of the hospital where my brother died, while Emily completes a scan, emotions I don't want to feel clawing and kicking inside me, demanding to be heard. It's almost like Derek's here with me. I feel him. God. I really do feel him. I stand up and walk to the reception desk. "I'm going around the corner to the coffee shop. I'll be back in ten minutes." I don't wait for a reply, exiting the waiting area and entering a familiar hallway I walked often while Derek and Emily were here. Memories start chattering in my head, and I flash back to Mike visiting the hospital, the reason I was out of the room when those alarms went off. I can see myself the moment they sounded. The next as I started running toward them. I can feel all over again how certain I was that either Derek or Emily had died.

I shake off the memory, rejecting it, and enter the coffee shop. The line is short and I order two coffees, one for me and one for Emily, and I'm not only back in the waiting room in a few minutes, I'm the only person occupying any of the two dozen or so chairs, leaving lots of empty space for my mind to fill. I hold my coffee, but I don't seem to be able to stomach it. I set it aside and rest my elbows on my knees, memories chattering in my head again. Inhaling, I straighten and fight the urge to pace, when I never pace. Pacing isn't about control. Pacing is about losing control.

I lean back in my seat and rest my head on the wall, shutting my eyes, the memories of the past refusing to be ignored. I'm back to those moments when I'd run toward the alarm.

I reach the doors of the hospital suite Emily and Derek are sharing, staff members blocking Emily's door. "I need inside!" I shout. "I need inside!"

A nurse turns to me, but right now I can't think of her name. "Shane—" she begins, but I cut her off.

"What's happening?"

"Emily's fine. She's absolutely fine."

Relief and heartache hit me in one breath. "My brother." It's not a question.

"They're working on him now," she assures me. "But we need you to wait outside the room."

"Emily needs me. She might wake up."

"She's still unconscious," she says. "It takes time for her to wake from the coma, which is normal."

"Shane!" I turn at the shout to find Teresa walking toward me, tears streaming down her face, her pain so damn palpable, it's like there's a living, breathing beast in the room.

I can't breathe. I can't move. I want to go to her, but it's as if my legs are now frozen. The world is spinning around me, and I watch as Teresa falls to her knees. Adrenaline surges through me and I am moving now, rushing toward her and screaming for help. Once again I'm pushed back by medical staff and I hear the word "shock." I'm not sure if they're talking about her or me.

Cody appears from I don't know where. He's speaking to me. Telling me about the sudden crash Derek has had, but I barely hear him. He's like a silent movie. His lips are moving, but no words are coming out. He's still moving his mouth when the doctor walks out of Derek's room and scans the hall, his gaze falling

on me, the look on his face telling me what on some level I al-
ready knew: Derek is gone.

I inhale and return to the present, aware that I've re-
played that memory with a version of me that was much
calmer than the day it happened, by at least 50 percent. I'd
been shouting and demanding. I'm pretty sure I shoved a cart at
some point. I'd been a crazy person who resembled nothing in
myself I know. That I've blocked that now, well, I'd like to
think that's my mind's way of telling me I'm halfway to sanity
again.

The doors to the treatment area open, and I'm on my
feet by the time Emily exits, a huge smile on her face. "I'm
clear. Today is a good day," she announces, wrapping her arms
around me.

"Yes," I say, stroking hair from her face. "It is." And as I
stand there, drowning in her pale blue eyes, I'm reminded that
the day I lost Derek was the day Emily came back to me. We
talk about a new beginning, but the truth is, that day was the
real new beginning.

Hours later Emily and I have long ago changed into jeans and
T-shirts to enjoy a night at home, which included takeout
from the restaurant we'd gone to the night we met. We've just
cleared our plates after finishing a meal of brown butter ravi-
oli, making room for the Macallan collector's edition box my
father gave me. "Now we celebrate," I say, setting it in front of
us, along with two glasses.

"It's almost too pretty to open," she says, running her
hand over the shiny black finish. "Shouldn't we collect a collector's edition?"

"We drink it with enough confidence to believe we deserve

every drop and can afford to buy another bottle every damn week if we want to."

"Confidence," she says. "I like that."

"Determination," I reply. "One of several gifts my father did give me."

She reaches over and strokes my sleeve upward, revealing my tattoo. "The eagle on the shoulders of the lion." And then she repeats the meaning I once shared with her: " 'The eagle is knowledge, strength, and leadership.' "

I finish the description for her. " 'And the lion is cunning and vicious. He'll rip your throat out if you give him the chance.' "

"And your father's the lion." She twists around to face me. "You're both the eagle and the lion now."

"Is that a good thing?"

"Yes. It is. Because you choose how and when to be those things, with the moral compass your father is missing."

My hand covers hers over my arm. "I'm a Brandon, Emily. You need to know that."

"And you've changed what that means. You need to know *that*."

"And what does that mean to you?"

"Everything."

I lean in to kiss her as the doorbell rings. "For a place with security," I say, "we get a lot of interruptions."

She sits up, tension radiating off of her. "It's about Rick." She looks at me. "It's about my brother. I don't know why, but I just know it is."

I stroke her hair. "Don't work yourself into fear. This is probably nothing." But as I stand and walk toward the foyer, her nerves become my adrenaline. I've lost a brother. I know the pain and do not wish this on Emily, and her pain is my fear.

The doorbell rings again and I stop at the door, steeling myself for a blow, not because it's logical, but because I can feel Emily behind me, waiting anxiously.

I unlock and open the door to find Seth standing in front of me, and the very fact that he's in jeans and a black polo tells me this isn't an expected visit. "I have news," he says, and now it's him with an envelope in his hand.

Backing up, I give him room to enter, and he joins me in the foyer, shutting the door behind him. His gaze immediately lands on Emily, as does mine, her face pale, expression tight. "I need to show you both something," Seth says, flicking a look between us.

I motion toward the kitchen and he walks under the archway to his right, headed in that direction. I hold out my hand to Emily. She walks forward and places her palm in mine but says nothing as I guide her to the island where we stand side by side across from Seth. He opens the envelope and tosses down a photo. "We found your brother."

Emily gasps and grabs the grainy photo, staring down at it and then looking at Seth. "Where was this? When was this?"

"In Germany. An hour ago."

"How did you find him in Germany?" Emily asks.

"A hacker he knows and trusts, a woman he has a relationship with actually, who also occasionally works for us, found him."

"He's alive," Emily breaths out. "Thank God, but . . . if you could find him, can't the Geminis?"

"They could," Seth agrees, "and he needs to be smarter to survive, but we've had our contractor create a scare for him and force him back underground. With us following him, of course, from this point forward. And knowing that he's in another country and pushed underground, we can be certain that our efforts to close the books on Reagan move forward without fear that he'll involve himself."

"So it's done," I say. "He's safe and he won't become a problem for us."

"He can't get to Emily without us knowing," Seth assures us. "This book is not closed, but we're the ones turning the pages." He sets the envelope on the table. "There are a few more shots inside that I'll leave." He turns to leave, but I pursue him, catching him at the door.

"Seth."

He turns to face me. I give him a nod meant to be a thank-you. He returns the nod and exits. I lock up and return to Emily, finding her still at the island, looking through several photos. "How do you feel?" I ask, joining her and turning her to face me.

"Relieved. Happy. He's not dead, but he's no longer the trouble for us that I feared. It's surreal. This is it. This was what we wanted and needed. This is me without security guards and—"

"Not quite yet," I say. "Let's allow everything to settle into place, but yes. We're almost there, as close to our normal as we're ever going to get. Tomorrow when we wake up, we start that new beginning. And now we celebrate." I scoop her up and forget the whiskey. I carry her upstairs to our bedroom, and already in my mind, I'm planning what I hadn't dared until now. How and when to ask her to be my wife.

PART TWO

NEW BEGINNINGS

EMILY

CHAPTER NINETEEN

There are times in our life when we face fear, and either we defeat it or it defeats us. Fear of life. Fear of death. The first time I experienced death was my father's suicide. I was angry with him. I was ashamed of him. I was angry with myself for not saving him. And then came the fear. Fear that I was his daughter, and therefore I would become him. Fear that I would never be loved, because if he loved me, he wouldn't have left me. Fear my mother was so distraught from his loss that she too would leave me. And she did. Years later, but she never recovered from his loss.

See, I believe that when fear controls us, it makes decisions for us. For my mother, fear chose my stepfather. Then my brother chose my stepfather. Then my mother was gone and I chose my brother, but he did not choose me. He turned on me. He deserted me. Shane chose his brother too, and ultimately his brother chose him when he chose me. That's hard to face sometimes. To know another person gave their life for your life. To know Shane looks at me and sees the woman who replaced his brother. Guilt and

*blame are almost as evil as fear. But Shane has never once acted
as if he blames me, and he seems to know when I blame me and
shuts it down. He doesn't let me feel those things, but his own feelings are another story. He feels guilt and blame, but that's where
I have to shut it down for him as well. Because I choose Shane.
And he chooses me.*

*I still think about my brother though, out there, in another
country. And I still feel fear. Maybe because this past month since
we found my brother, life has been almost too good. Shane and I
have fallen into routines together that we enjoy. We endure random encounters with his parents together. We get excited and
angry over business together. We celebrate success together. I think
he was as excited or even more so when I managed to recruit the
Luc Monroe, who has designed for two of the largest brands in the
world, to join our operation.*

*Some part of me feels like what we share is too good to be
true. Like Shane will be ripped away from me, the way so many
things in my life have been ripped away from me.*

The private jet Shane chartered for us to fly from Denver
to Manhattan begins to descend, and I shut my new journal that
I bought at the airport a few hours ago, nervous and excited
about our arrival. "I can't believe I'm about to be in New York
City," I say, "experiencing your alternate universe. And that
we're going to visit our designer at his proposed flagship Fifth
Avenue store."

"Alternate universe?" Shane laughs, our jean-clad knees
pressed together; his are faded, low-hung, and sexy, while mine
are simply black. "Sweetheart," he adds, his hand settling on
my thigh, "there's no alternate universe. There is just the one
we're living inside together."

"Now," I say. "But we're entering a place that was your world
before me. The one you, rather than your father, created."

"This is our world," he reiterates. "The one where we have apartments in Denver and New York, and a business that favors an operation in both cities." He taps the journal in my hand. "You've been writing nonstop in that thing since you picked it up in the airport. What has you so inspired?"

"I've kept a journal since my father died," I say, sticking it inside my oversized black Chanel satchel purse that I've come to favor these past few weeks because it doubles as a briefcase if I really organize well. "I guess I missed the therapy and creativity it represents more than I realized."

"I hate to bring this up, sweetheart, but you know—"

"Not to write about Reagan or anything related to Reagan. I know. It's mostly just my feelings anyway."

"Feelings?" He arches a brow. "Anything I should be concerned about?"

"You can read it if you want and decide for yourself."

"That's your private escape," he says without any hesitation, "and if anyone deserves that, it's you. Besides I'd rather you tell me, and *show me*, what you're feeling."

My lips curve. "Show not tell?"

"I like it when you show *and* tell."

I laugh, but a thought hits me and my eyes go wide. "My old journals," I say, twisting around to face him. "I wrote information about my brother and stepfather in them. About the Geminis. What if that has law enforcement hunting for them?"

"Reagan's death was ruled an overdose," he says, "so I doubt they read those journals, but we'll text Seth." He grabs his phone from the drink holder next to him and sends a text message. He hands me the phone to allow me to read what he's typed, and Seth answers as he does: *All of Emily's things are in our possession, to be returned to her in the next few weeks. I'm not aware of any journals the police investigated at all. It's a non-issue.*

"There you go," Shane says, slipping his phone into his pocket and then squeezing my leg. "Don't start creating a problem where there isn't one. We're past that."

"And yet you still have Cody following me around in Denver?"

His gray eyes darken, those shadows I find lurking in their depths overtaking the blue flecks too often these days. "Let's consider this weekend a trial run without him." The plane comes to a halt, the engines' roars turning to purrs. "And we're here." He unhooks his belt, drags a hand through his thick, dark hair, and stands up.

I unbuckle myself but remain sitting, watching first as the doors open, an airport staffer entering the plane. The man seems to know Shane, waving at him and closing the space between us. The thirtysomething man, in a logoed collar shirt, gives me a mock salute and then refocuses on Shane. "Good to see you, man."

"Good to see you too, John," Shane greets him, shaking the other man's hand, and it's clear there was a time that Shane chartered planes on at least a semi-regular basis.

"What can I get for you?" John asks.

"We have a couple bags here," Shane says, reaching into the overhead bin, while I find myself watching him, my mind troubled by those shadows in his eyes. My eyes are not at all troubled by the stretch of his tan UFC T-shirt across his broad chest and the way his sleeve tugs higher with the flex of his biceps, displaying the tattoo of the eagle sitting on top of the lion on his right shoulder. It hits me then that beyond the meaning he's shared with me about knowledge and force, it's ultimately symbolic of him rising above his father, and even his family name. Something he did by separating himself from them and coming here, among many other things.

I consider his "trial run" comment again, regarding the prospect of life without Cody following us around, and it hits me that if Shane feels comfortable without security here, and not in Denver, *our home*, we have a problem. Maybe there's danger in Denver he hasn't shared with me, but more likely, I think, the very idea of Adrian Martina, and even his father, being a stone's throw from us is never going to allow him peace. And that too is a problem we have to solve. I just need to find the right moment to dive into that dark psyche of his and take a long swim.

Shane reaches for my hand, drawing it into his. And just like that, he's successfully wiped out my worry, a shiver racing up my spine that has nothing to do with my bare arms in my thin black V-neck T-shirt, and everything to do with his touch.

"Let the adventure begin," he murmurs, kissing my knuckles.

I smile, seduced by the idea of an adventure with this man, and even more so by finally discovering part of him I know but have never fully realized. The eagle, not the lion. He helps me to my feet. I settle my purse on my arm and, with his urging, step into the aisle before him. His hand is instantly at my waist, and he is close, kissing my neck from behind before he whispers, "Your ass looks really good in those black jeans." He follows that declaration by smacking my new pancake-plumped backside that he seems to love, or I'd have already started running every mile it will take to shed it.

Nevertheless, I yelp with the sting on my cheek that he's intentionally created, and move toward the exit. Stepping to the doorway, I feel suffocated by the late June New York heat. "It's like being back in Texas," I say as Shane steps to my side.

"I don't miss the heat," he says, but there is this silent inference that he misses everything else, or something else I don't try to name now, but I will, or rather he will, before we leave.

Side by side, we start down the ramp when a limo pulls forward. "That would be our car," he says.

"A limo? We need a limo?"

"It's your first time in New York," he says. "It needs to be in style. And it has a big trunk for our bags. You packed a lot of shoes."

"That was Jessica," I say, leaving the steps. "I should never have let her help me pack. I didn't even buy those shoes. She did with your credit card."

"Which is why we're going to go shopping while we're here and you can choose your own clothes." It turns out John is our driver, and he holds the back door open for us. "And I'm paying."

"Shane—"

He arches a brow, and I become aware of John staring at us. I bite back my words and save them for inside the limo, sliding inside, the tan leather seats a box that lines the back of the vehicle. A bucket of champagne on ice is in the center. Shane joins me and John shuts us inside, a glass window sealed between us and the front of the vehicle.

"I don't need you to buy everything for me," I tell him.

He fills two glasses and hands one to me. "Save your money so if you ever get pissed and want to leave me, you and I both know you can."

"We both know?"

"That's right. It's good for us to both know you can leave. Because you can. I just don't want you to. Ever, Emily."

My heart squeezes with the rough quality to his voice, and

I'm not sure if he's talking about fights and relationship troubles, or rather death. I'm not sure what to say, because telling him I want to be here won't erase the real, festering root of that comment.

"I still want you to know that I don't expect you to take care of me," I say. "I never want you to feel like—"

"You want my money? Sweetheart, if you wanted money, you would have jumped on your stepfather's bandwagon. He had money. I have money. I've told you this, and I worked damn hard for it, for us."

"For you."

"For my future, which you are." His voice softens. "We share a life, Emily. I want to share all of it with you. I have never wanted that with anyone else. I love you, Emily."

Emotion wells in my throat. "I love you too, Shane."

He lifts his glass. "To our first of many travel adventures."

I touch my glass to his. "To our first—of many?"

"Of many," he says, clicking his glass to mine. "Where do you want to go next?"

"I think right now I just want to enjoy this trip, and your city, through your eyes."

"Our city," he corrects me again, "and I'll learn to appreciate it all over again through your eyes."

We spend the next two hours driving around Manhattan, sipping our champagne and talking, taking in everything from Times Square to Rockefeller Center and much more before we finally end at Shane's apartment building, an all-glass highrise across from Central Park. John opens the door for us and I step outside, staring up at the building, which has a central structure and two towers behind it.

Shane settles up with John, having a conversation about

our bags and the doorman before he steps to my side. "The building on the right is residential. The building on the left has office complexes and shopping." He guides me forward and greets the doorman, who seems to know him well, but Shane doesn't seem eager to get drawn into a conversation. Shane palms him money to deliver our bags to the apartment, and I'm introduced to a security guard, who motions us inside. We step into the building, the tiles shiny gray with swirls, the ceilings high, the lights dangling every few feet, like stars in a dark sky.

A few minutes later I'm registered as a tenant, which is rather surreal, and Shane is holding my hand, leading me into an elevator. We enter, and he punches the twenty-eighth floor before pulling me and motioning to the back of the elevator. My brow furrows in confusion until we start moving and the wall is gone, and I realize that the car is all glass. I'm now staring across Central Park and the Manhattan skyline behind it, with its jutted rooftops of various heights and colors.

"This is amazing," I say, glancing over at him. "Though if I were afraid of heights, I'd have face-planted into your shoulder."

He laughs. "I've actually seen that a few times."

"How long have you owned this apartment?"

"Five years."

The elevator dings behind us and we rotate, exiting the car hand in hand as we hit the tiled walkway and cut right. "Here," he says, of the double doors on the right, halting to punch in a code. He opens the door and motions me forward.

"Your real home," I say, starting forward, but Shane catches my hand and turns me to him.

"I never called it home," he says. "I never called any place home before you, so turn this place into something more than it is."

I wonder if he's trying to convince me or himself, but I don't say that. Not yet. Not when he hasn't been back here in months and can't really know what returning will feel like and what it means to him. Right now he's just thinking of me, which makes him pretty amazing, but that means I need to be amazing to him too. And no one else in his life is amazing to him besides Jessica, which only makes me love her more. So my reply is not words. I lean forward, hand on his heart, and I feel it thunder beneath my palm, telling me he's more affected than he wants me, and himself, to realize.

I lean into him and push to my toes, pressing my lips to his. He cups my head in that familiar way he does, and his tongue strokes against mine, a slow, sexy caress that ends too soon, leaving us both breathing just a little harder. Slowly, we ease apart, our eyes lingering the way our lips had, the connection broken only when I turn away and walk through the doorway, a dark wooden floor beneath my booted feet. Much like in our Denver apartment, I walk down a long hallway, but this one is narrower, the ceiling above curved, creating a tunneled effect, and when I exit, I gasp at the sights before me and around me.

I am standing in a stunning contemporary space that seems to go on forever both to my left and right, the décor done in grays and blues, with clean, simple shapes and lines that also manage to be elegant. Windows, not walls, encase the room, the design managing to create a feeling of being in the sky, floating on air, while two huge pillars split the living and dining areas. A staircase to the right follows windows upstairs, and one to the left heads to a lower level.

"What do you think?" Shane asks, stepping to my side.

"It makes the Denver apartment look uninteresting, and yet the Denver apartment isn't uninteresting at all." My gaze travels the skyline, the sun beginning to set, creating a halo effect above the buildings. "And I thought Denver was beautiful."

"It is, but Manhattan's skyline is its answer to the Rocky Mountains. Come," he says, linking our fingers. "I want to show you my favorite part of the apartment." He leads me to the stairs to our left, and my hand skims a stainless steel railing while steps of the same dark wood as the floor lead us to an office with a vaulted, completely glass ceiling that I am certain must be our destination.

But we don't stop there.

He motions for me to walk up a narrow stairwell in the center of the room, and something about his energy has me excited to get to the top. I quickly move ahead of him and climb the narrow path, stepping into a cubbyhole of sorts, encased in glass, that fits only two cozy overstuffed chairs and a small table.

"My thinking room," he says, joining me, his head nearly touching the glass ceiling. "And the reason I bought this apartment." His fingers lace with mine and we step to the window, the sky now blue, orange, and yellow. "It's like you're on top of the world," he says.

"I want to sit in this room with coffee and a book and stay for hours."

"I've done that many times," he says, turning to me, his hands settling on my waist. "Emily."

"Shane," I say, suddenly nervous and I don't know why.

"When I thought of the way I wanted this weekend to happen, I knew we needed to be someplace that didn't surround us with tragedy."

"It feels different here, doesn't it?"

"Yes. It does. I knew it would, but I also knew you'd associate this place with my past, and I worried that you'd decide I would rather be living my old life, not my new life. So to be clear: my past made me the man I had to be to face what was waiting for me in Denver. It made me the man I needed to be when I met you. The man who I am right now. The man who fell in love with you. That's why I wanted to do this here."

"Do what? You're scaring me."

He laughs without humor. "Then this is really not going the way I planned, so let me just get to the point." He goes down on his knee. "Marry me, Emily."

Shock rolls through me. "What? I . . . Yes. No. Oh God. *No.* You can't marry me."

"I assure you I can and will. *If* you say yes. Let me re-phrase: Will you marry me, Emily?"

"But I'm not Emily. I'm Reagan. What if the marriage license application exposes that somehow?"

He pushes to his feet and cups my face. "You are Emily, and I swear to you that one day, if you let me, I'm going to make sure you don't react to everything with the fear you do now. *Marry me, Emily.*" He reaches to the table and then goes down on his knee again, opening a blue Tiffany's box.

I gasp at the sight of a stunning heart-shaped diamond that glistens almost blue in the lights. "It's incredible," I whisper.

"This is where you say yes, sweetheart."

I start crying and go down on my knees with him. "Yes."

He reaches over and strokes tears from my cheeks. "Why are you crying? Please tell me it's not fear. I promise you—"

"It's not fear. These are happy tears, and don't ask me to explain what happy tears are because I really don't know. They just are what they are."

"Then let's let them exist with your ring on your finger." He removes the ring from the velvet and sets the box aside before slipping the ring on my finger. "It's a little big," he says, "but we'll size it."

"It's perfect and it's not big." I forget the ring and press my lips to his.

He lays us on the floor, and only then do I realize there is a fluffy, soft rug beneath us, while the stars and sky are above us. "Emily Brandon," he says, his leg twining with mine. "I like the way that sounds." He strokes hair from my face. "I love you, woman."

"I love you too." My fingers curl on his jaw. "I've never had anyone I trust like you. I've never had anyone I . . . trust. Trust says it all. You even told me when you wanted to kill Martina, when I know you knew how I'd react."

"That wasn't completely honorable. There was a part of me that wanted to scare you off if you couldn't handle who I really am."

"Good thing I know who you really are," I say, "because you seem to think you're your father's son."

His voice sobers. "I am my father's son, Emily."

"But you are also your own man. The one I love."

He studies me for several beats, those shadows in his eyes still there, but when he kisses me, I taste the bad still haunting him, and I let him taste the bad that still haunts me. And that's where I got it wrong in my journal. I thought we were too good to be true. But we aren't. And I know this because when he strips me naked, and I strip him naked, it's more than physical. We bare it all, and that makes me believe that maybe, just maybe, we can have it all.

CHAPTER TWENTY

I wake the next morning in a massive four poster bed, facing a wall of windows that are all electronically shaded, with Shane curled around me and a Tiffany's engagement ring on my finger. Life is good, and I close my eyes, not quite ready to get up. It just feels too good to be right here, right now. I snuggle closer to Shane and allow myself to drift back to sleep. The next time I blink awake, the windows are no longer shaded and Shane is no longer in bed with me. I sit up straight and Shane is sitting next to me, fully dressed in a gray suit with a blue pinstripe and a navy-blue tie. "Why are you awake, dressed, and holding coffee while I'm in bed, in a robe, and not holding coffee?"

His lips curve. "The coffee is for you," he says, offering it to me. "And I have some work I have to finish up, then I can focus on the fashion brand with you today." He glances at his watch. "We have an hour before we need to leave to meet the Realtor to look at the proposed store location." He reaches down and takes my hand, studies my ring, then without another word, stands up and leaves.

I watch him leave, and sigh with satisfaction at the realization that not only is he sexy, intelligent, and protective without being obnoxious, he's going to be my husband. I sip from my cup approvingly and add: he also makes a really good cup of coffee. I carry it with me to the stunning window-framed bathroom, vowing to take a bath while looking out over the city. Because who doesn't want to take a bath with a sweeping view of the city, and bubbles that might just be clouds?

Laughing at the silly idea that proves I'm a little giddy this morning, I enjoy another sip of my coffee, strip away my gown, and take a quick hot shower. My relaxed mood continues through the process of drying my hair and flat-ironing it to a sleek, shiny finish, and applying makeup in pale pinks. I head into the giant closet that's the size of my bedroom back in Texas, or maybe actually bigger than my bedroom back in Texas, and open my suitcase, pulling out my choices for the day, and it's then that my nerves kick in. I'm going to meet our new famous fashion designer in person for the first time today. What if he judges me incapable of running a fashion brand because my personal style is lacking?

I have three outfits with me, all of which Jessica chose when Shane sent her shopping for me, but they're high-fashion brands, and beautiful. I decide on a light blue dress with a matching belt, nude hose and shoes, and once everything is on, I study myself in the mirror. What if light blue isn't an approved New York fashion color? I strip it away and choose a black skirt and a black silk blouse, which means black shoes and hose, but as I inspect myself, I question black as a June color. The only thing I have left is the pale pink dress Shane really likes on me, but pink ages me young, and I'm not sure that works for my first meeting with someone reporting to me.

"Problem?"

I rotate to find Shane leaning against the doorway while I stand in the center of the closet in a black bra, panties, and black thigh-highs. All of which he gives a wicked hot inspection, and I force myself to ignore the wicked hot heat it stirs in me in response.

"I want to look like I know fashion and that I know my job. I'm not sure which of my three outfits to wear."

"Which is your favorite?"

"The pink."

"Then wear the pink and own it like you would a courtroom." He walks to me and cups my face. "You're the boss," he says. "Remember that. That's an order." He then plants a kiss on me, releases me, and exits the closet.

"I'm the boss but that's an order?" I call after him, but I've already absorbed his message and I'm reaching for the pink dress. He's right. *I am* the boss, and I have to own this job the way I would have a courtroom.

The rest of the day is incredible, both professionally and personally. The retail location is perfect, and we sign a lease. Since it's right across from Tiffany's, Shane and I stop inside. One of the Tiffany's employees adds some sort of spacer to my ring, and it now fits perfectly. Afterward, we head to the fashion district and spend the rest of the day with our new designer, mapping out plans, staffing, and setting a launch date of spring. About an hour into our meetings, the designer pushes to move manufacturing to New York, but Shane nixes that idea; based on labor and real estate operational costs, we've already purchased a Castle Rock, Colorado, production facility as part of our acquisition. Even so, it's still quite clear that much of the business side of things will be rooted in New York and I'll have to travel back and forth between there and Colorado.

By late afternoon we've changed into jeans again, and Shane wants to show me the city. So we start walking, and the hours that follow include talking, eating, and just being together. The sun is starting to set when we arrive back at our building, and Shane suggests we stop in a wine bar in the second tower. We head that way and claim a table by a window that allows us a view of the horses and carriages lined up along Central Park.

"What kind of wine would you like?" he asks, glancing at the menu.

"Surprise me," I say. "It will be fun to try something new."

Those blue flecks in his gray eyes light with approval, but when the first glass of wine arrives, it's dry and bitter, and my nose crinkles of its own accord. He laughs and motions for the waiter. "This time you sample first."

I sample four wines to finally find one that I like, but once I receive the full glass, my stomach rumbles loudly before I ever take a sip. Shane grins and slides the bowl of candy-coated nuts that came on our table in front of me. "I'd say that's a sign we should get the check, and we can either go somewhere to eat or order in."

"Order in," I say. "I'm kind of obsessed with that apartment."

"Shane?"

I glance up to find a good-looking man with salt-and-pepper hair, in an obviously expensive brown suit with a hint of red plaid in it that matches his tie. "Freddy," Shane says, standing to shake his hand.

"Why didn't you tell me you were in town?" Freddy asks, unbuttoning his jacket to slide his hands to his lean waist. "You know the firm is a few floors up in this very building."

My eyes go wide. "The firm is here?"

"It is," Freddy says, eying Shane. "You told her about the firm but not that it's in this building. Interesting. I repeat: Why didn't you call? You know you wanted to call."

"The location of the firm is irrelevant," Shane says. "And you know why I didn't call. Nothing has changed."

"But it has." Freddy looks in my direction. "You have a new companion, who is quite lovely, I might add."

My cheeks heat. "Thank you."

"Emily," Shane says. "This is my ex-boss, Freddy Woods, but we call him Maverick in the courtroom. And Freddy, this is Emily Stevens, who is soon to be Emily Brandon."

Freddy arches a brow at Shane. "Engaged. Another interesting development. Now I know who to plead my case to." He shifts his gaze back to me. "Nice to meet you, Emily." He grabs a chair and pulls it to the end of the table. "How do you feel about New York?"

"I love it," I say, glancing at Shane, who reclaims his seat and says, "What he's doing right now is why I didn't call him."

"How do you feel about *living* in New York?" Freddy asks, still focusing on me, ignoring Shane.

"Rein it in, Maverick," Shane warns.

"You want him to come back to work for you?" I ask. "I mean, that's the obvious message here, right?"

"I want him to do more than come back to work for us," Freddy says. "I want him to be the youngest partner in our history."

My gaze jerks to Shane's, a question in my eyes.

"He knows I have a company to run," Shane replies.

"And I also know," Freddy interjects, "that you're too damn good in a courtroom to stay away." He looks between us. "I don't want to interrupt your night out, but Shane," he adds, refocusing on him, "let's set a time to talk before you leave. Give me an hour to pitch an idea I have to make this work."

"Why don't you two talk now?" I suggest quickly, knowing that Shane wants to hear what Freddy has to say, even if he won't admit it to himself. And what he wants I want, and I don't see why he can't have the best of both worlds anyway, past and present. Given the way things have unfolded.

"I don't want to interrupt any more than I have," Freddy says.

"Nonsense," I say, glancing at the clock on my phone. "I have a lifetime with Shane, and I also have just enough time to sneak to the mall in the building." I slide my purse to my shoulder and stand. Shane doesn't look pleased, and I can almost see him sway, ready to stand and halt my departure. "There's no reason to worry," I say, trying to remind him we're past our troubles. "I won't torture you with shopping. I'll be back at the apartment long before you two are done, I'm sure. I'll text you so you don't have to hunt me down."

"Looks like you got yourself a keeper here, Shane," Freddy says. "My wife expects me to grin and bear it." He gives me a smile. "Thank you, Emily. I'll try to make this worth your while."

"Make it worth Shane's," I say. "Not mine." I look at Shane, making sure he's okay with my plan here, not because he's the boss of me in some way, but because, the truth is, the loss of his brother is still too recent not to be raw. Shane is slow to respond, probably reminding himself of all the reasons danger is behind me, and us, but finally he nods. "The escalators will take you to the mall."

"Got it," I say. "I'll text you," I repeat, and turn away before he can change his mind.

Exiting the bar, I enter the main lobby of the building to

find it busy, people hustling and bustling here and there. Scanning, I find the escalator and start walking, noting the coffee shop, gift shop, and mail store on the lower level with interest, considering it looks like we may be here often. I've just stepped onto the escalator when an odd sense of unease rolls through me, which I quickly attribute to being out on my own for the first time in months. Still, I find myself twisting around to look behind me, discovering the closest person to me to be a couple of teenagers who are chattering to themselves and have no interest in me.

I exit the escalator and discover brand-name stores left and right, as well as another escalator to stores up another level. Since I really have no specific item I'm looking for, I decide to just stroll and see what draws my attention. I wander in and out of stores and grab a couple small items. a T-shirt that catches my eye. A few toiletry items. An eye shadow palette I love, my mind already thinking of our makeup line, which I hope to launch right after the fashion line. Each time I enter a store, that weird feeling eases just a little. Each time I step back into the public area, it screams a little louder in my head.

It's really crazy, though. The mall isn't that busy. And I'm in jeans and a T-shirt, only my Chanel purse worthy of attention at all. The unease is really working me over, though, and I'm about to head to the apartment when I pass a Swarovski store and spot a gorgeous miniature crystal lion in the window. I immediately halt and then enter the store, and the instant I discover they also have an eagle, I break out the credit card in my wallet.

Excited about my gifts for Shane, I am done shopping and I make my way down the escalator, but as I step into the busy lobby, that uneasy feeling becomes almost tangible. With no easy connection from tower to tower to see, despite knowing it must exist, I cross to the front door and exit to the street, only to be rammed by someone. I gasp and stumble, a stranger catching my arm. "Are you okay?"

I blink up at the tall, muscular man with dark hair and eyes. "Yes," I say. "Thank you." But that uneasy feeling is back, and I pull my arm away, dart around him, and hurry several feet to enter the apartment building.

Once I'm in the lobby, I juggle the awkwardness of my bags and all but run to the elevators. I'm quickly inside a car on my way to our floor, choosing to ignore the view behind me to watch the doors, the time ticking by in what feels like slow motion. I pull my phone out of my purse, but I don't text Shane yet. I just want to be in the apartment first. The doors open, and I rush into the hallway, wasting no time covering the distance to our door and keying in the code. The door pops right open, but I start thinking about the Geminis and how easy it would be for someone like my brother to hack that code. That thought makes it really hard for me to enter the apartment, but the hallway isn't much better, and I'm just making myself crazy. Everyone in that world thinks I'm dead.

I think of the fear I wrote about in my journal and how easily it can consume those it has found. It can't consume me. It can't win. I text Shane: *I'm walking into the apartment now.* I shove open the door. Flipping on the light, I walk inside and lock the door. I stand there, listening for anything that sounds wrong, but I hear nothing. I feel nothing, I realize. That uneasy feeling is gone. I press my hand to my face. Have I developed some sort of paranoia? Please no. Tell me no. No! I have not. Shane and I are both just letting recent events control us. We have to talk about this and get over it together, or we'll keep re-creating it in each other.

I push off the door and walk down the hallway, entering

the living and dining area. Scanning to be safe, I see nothing odd and feel nothing odd. Tension uncurls in my belly and shoulders, and I head to my left and down the hallway. Entering the master bedroom, I flip on the lights, inhaling the familiar spice in the air that is so Shane, and walk to the bathroom to repeat the process. My final stop is the closet, where I deposit my bags. Retrieving the gifts for Shane from one of them, I remove them from the boxes and return to the bedroom to set them on the nightstand by his side of the bed.

Excited for the moment he spots them, I return to the bathroom, start running a hot bath, and add sweet floral bubbles I bought at the mall to the water. A few minutes later I am naked in the tub, my journal on the slender table that runs between the tub and the window. But instead of writing, I stare out at the city lights speckling the now dark sky, and I have this sense of being where I belong. Where Shane and I belong, which is why I hate that I had that mini freak-out while shopping. I don't want to create worry in Shane. My brother is not an issue anymore. And Martina isn't here. Mike Rogers isn't here. Shane's father isn't here. This is our place.

The sound of the door opening and shutting fills the air, and I can hear Shane's steady, confident footsteps. A full minute, maybe two, later, he appears in the doorway, his expression unreadable, heavy, dark, like his energy, those broken pieces I'd written about yesterday almost certainly cutting him, and deeply. He wants to be here in this city, doing the legal work he loves. He thinks he can't, but never do I think this is about me holding him back. This is about him and, knowing him, I don't ask questions. He's not ready to talk.

As if driving home that point, his eyes glint and he pulls his shirt over his head. Adrenaline rushes through me, and in moments he's naked too, his hard, long lean body perfection, his shaft jutting forward. I sit up, exposing my naked, wet breasts. His gaze rakes over them, hot and hungry, and before I know his intent, he's pulling me to my feet, his arm wrapping around my waist, and he drags me to him and out of the tub. Water pools at our feet, but he doesn't seem to care. His fingers are tangled in my hair. His hands cup my breasts, fingers teasing my nipples. And when his tongue licks into my mouth, I can taste the demand, the hunger that he needs to feed.

He turns us and sets me on the counter, his lips lifting from mine, his breath mingling with mine, but he doesn't linger. His fingers stroke into my sex, and when I expect his urgency, him inside me, that's not what happens. He's suddenly on his knees, spreading my legs, his mouth on my clit like he needs to own my pleasure, to control me right now. But it's not about me and I know this, though, oh God. The strokes of his tongue, his fingers inside me, feels . . . a lot about me right . . . now. I am so close to—

His mouth and fingers are suddenly gone, and he's standing. "You come with me." He presses inside me, filling me, stretching me, and he's so damn hard, it's brutal, sweet, bliss. He drives deep, tangling his fingers in my hair, and his mouth closes down on me, the taste of him now salty, sweet, me. It's what he wants, I think. It's about control, I think again, his hand splaying between my shoulder blades, his lips torn from mine as he cups my backside and lifts me. I think he will hold me, fuck me, right there, but instead he carries me to the bedroom, settling me on my back and him on top. He rolls and pulls me on top of him.

"Ride me, sweetheart," he orders softly.

I sit up, his hands anchoring me at my hips, his gaze hot all over again. I'm hot all over again. He watches me. Every sway of my breasts. Every thrust of my hips. I lean back, my hands on his legs, and he sits up, cupping my breasts, stroking them. His hand is back between my shoulder blades, bracing me as his lips and tongue tease my nipples. Kissing them. Kissing me, and he tastes different now. Still dark, but more passionate in his demand. I wrap my arms around his neck and he buries his face in mine and we rock and sway into that place of no return. Until we are both trembling. Quaking. I collapse against him, and he holds me but doesn't move. For a full minute we sit there, in the aftermath, and I think of what brought us here tonight and long before.

I push back, my hands on his shoulders, and look at him. "Talk to me. Tell me about the meeting with Freddy."

"There's nothing to tell." He rolls me to my back. "He wants me back. I said no." He glances at the nightstand. "The lion and the eagle."

"You," I say. "They're both you. And you can be those things here."

"I love the gift, Emily, and what you are trying to do, but I said no to his offer." He pulls out of me. "I'll get you a towel." He walks to the bathroom, and I scramble to the nightstand, grab a tissue, quickly right myself, and pursue him.

I reach him as he appears in the doorway, his jeans back on, low-slung and unzipped, a towel in his hand. "We can live here. The company looks different now. It can work and work well with the fashion brand."

"My father is still terminal. At any moment I can get pulled back there."

"Not to run a company."

"We have a board."

"That just wants to make money. Keep the fashion brand. Make that Brandon Enterprises. And you take the partner role at your firm."

"It's not my firm, but Brandon Enterprises is my company. I can't be an active partner in any firm and be CEO of ours."

"We can find a way to make it work. I know we can."

He picks me up, sets me on the counter, then grabs my robe from behind the door and slides it around me. I push my arms into the sleeves and he ties the sash. "Let's order dinner."

I want to push him to talk about this, more so to take this job, but I sense that's not what he needs from me right now. "Let's order dinner," I agree instead, and not long after, we settle into the room where he proposed, his—now *our*— "thinking room," and when we're done stuffing our faces with Chinese food, we lie on our backs and stare at the sky, counting stars. Sensing the rough edges of his mood have softened, I dare to ask, "Why do you call Freddy 'Maverick'?"

To my pleasure, he laughs and glances over at me. "Because it's better than calling him 'dumbass.' "

I laugh now too. "He didn't seem dumb at all. He wants to hire you again and make you partner."

"Because he needs someone to save his dumb ass."

"Okay, tell me what that means."

"He goes at cases in ways that make not one bit of fucking sense, and I'm always sure he'll end up dead or at least bleeding. But he doesn't break the law in the process and his unorthodox ways always work for him. I swear, the man has some voodoo magic working for him."

"You admire him," I observe.

He surprises me by saying, "He's the man my father could have been but chose not to be."

I reach up and stroke his jaw, and I want to push him again. I do. So very badly, but I still sense it's not the right time. "Tell me more about this voodoo," I say. "Maybe we can use it to make the fashion brand do magic of its own."

I sense him relax with that question, and instead of struggling through his decision to leave his legal career behind a second time, we talk for hours, his stories of Freddy morphing into us talking about crazy things that happened to Shane in the courtroom and with clients. And he's different when he talks about that world, right in ways that I now realize Brandon Enterprises is wrong for him. He knows this too. I know he does. His rejection of Freddy's offer isn't about a legal issue that we both know he's capable of handling. I wonder if, subconsciously, saying good-bye to Denver is like saying the good-bye to Derek he never got to say. And once you say good-bye, the loss is final.

I think my brother said good-bye to me before he ever heard I was dead.

CHAPTER TWENTY-ONE

I go to bed that night with Shane wrapped around me, holding me almost too tight. He doesn't sleep. I don't sleep. For a long time we just lie there, listening to each other think without sharing our actual thoughts. I wake the next morning at sunrise to the same, Shane holding me, and us both in deep thought. And with the knowledge that we leave for Denver, *for home*, at two. Only it doesn't feel like home. It feels like a necessary destination on our path to here.

"Let's go run in Central Park," Shane says, kissing my neck, and just like that we're up, and within half an hour we're running off the heaviness of our combined moods, engaged in the energy of the many other morning joggers.

We return to the apartment by nine, shower together to save time, and both of us throw on jeans and T-shirts for comfort; we're packed by ten. I, of course, choose an I ♥ NEW YORK T-shirt and point it out to Shane as we head to the elevator, as if he can't see it himself. "Because I love New York."

"We'll be back," he promises, "but if you want to be a

New Yorker, you can never, ever wear that shirt again. It's a tourist shirt."

"Make me a New Yorker and I won't dress like a tourist."

We step into the elevator, and he punches the lobby level before pulling me close. "How about I just make you my wife?"

"Does it come with a T-shirt?"

The elevator stops on a random floor, the doors opening, and several people enter. Shane scoots me into a corner and leans in close to whisper, "No shirt," he says, a sexy suggestive curve to his lips. "Just me. Is the deal off?"

"I really wanted the shirt," I whisper, heat simmering between us for no reason other than we're us.

And I really love that we're us. I love that we laugh together. I love that at the airport, he orders coffee for me and doesn't even ask what I want. He just knows. And I love that when we settle into our seats on the private jet he's chartered, and open our laptops, we're just as comfortable talking together as not talking at all, both of us trying to get lost in work. What I don't love is the way that heaviness before our run returns as the engines roar to life, announcing our return to Denver.

I consider talking to Shane about it, but he's immersed in a contract he's reviewing, and I have to review the transition staffing reports from HR, or that's my intent. Once we're airborne, I log on to the internet to download the documents, and Jessica sends me an instant message: *How did it go with the designer?*

I glance at Shane. "How does Jessica even know the minute I log on to the internet on a Sunday?"

"She's a professional stalker and I actually pay her to do it," he says. "And give her bonuses in expensive brand-name clothing that usually comes with a Chanel label, as if I endorse the behavior."

"Which reminds me," I say. "We need to talk to her about her Jessica label. We told the designer about it. Jessica needs to know and get involved."

"Agreed," he says, and before returning to our work, we decide on tomorrow morning at the office coffee shop to talk to her.

I chat with Jessica in messenger for a few minutes, filling her in on the trip. Typing my replies, my eyes fall on my ring, and I realize Jessica is really the only person I have to share the news with, a thought that stirs memories of my mother, which I quickly shove away. I don't tell Jessica about the ring. I decide I'll show her tomorrow instead. I disconnect with her and quickly engage myself in work rather than emotions, struggling with some eye strain and dizziness the entire time. Deciding I need to see the eye doctor, I store my computer and try to use my journal for notes, but the same issue replays. We're descending when the dizziness becomes something much worse. My stomach rolls and I unbuckle myself to rush around Shane to the back of the plane, where the door jams.

Shane is there almost immediately, grabbing my arm as the plane jolts and saving me from a certain tumble. "I've got you," he says, "and the door." He reaches for the handle.

I lean against the door. "Never mind."

He arches a brow. "Never mind?"

"I was feeling what I guess was motion sickness, but I'm not anymore."

"You've never mentioned motion sickness."

"I've never felt it before. Maybe it was the wine last night."

"You hardly drank any of it."

"But it was very strong," I argue.

He laughs. "*You* are drunk *right now*." He grabs my hand and leads me back to my seat, and we've barely buckled up when we hit the runway. Shane's phone buzzes instantly.

He reads the text message and looks at me. "Cody is waiting for us on the tarmac."

"Cody." I sigh. "We're back to our bodyguard."

Shane's hand comes down on my leg. "Emily—"

"I know. You want to protect me, and I'm not complaining about you caring. But I just want you to think about the implication of what you just said. In New York you were okay with us having no bodyguard. Here, you're not."

"Martina's here."

"Exactly," I say softly. "He's here. Why do we want to be here if we're worried enough to need security? It's affecting me. I felt paranoid at the mall yesterday. I kept looking over my shoulder."

He straightens. "Why didn't you tell me this before now?"

"It was just last night," I say. "And I really think I was just paranoid. I don't want to be conditioned to be afraid to be alone."

"It's only been two months since your attack," he says. "It's impossible for you to be at ease, and me to not feel protective. We need to talk about it like we are now."

"Agreed," I say. "But we said we wanted a new beginning."

"You really want to move to New York, don't you?"

"Don't you?"

He surprises me by saying, "Yes, but moving there is complicated."

"Isn't staying here as well?"

The door to the cabin opens, and Cody walks in, his presence driving home the accuracy of my question with far more than words. For us, being in Denver means danger.

It's an hour later when we arrive at our building in downtown Denver and make our way to our apartment to find a note on the door that reads: *Delivery left in the kitchen.*

"That's curious," I say. "What is it?"

"Probably just too much mail for the box," Shane says, crumpling the note and stuffing it into his pocket before opening the door.

Movement behind us has us both turning to find the doorman walking toward us, our bags on a cart. "The perks of living in a hotel," Shane murmurs.

I leave him to deal with our bags, entering the apartment, my intention to find out what was left in the kitchen. But as I step into the foyer, memories assail me, and I find myself standing at the edge of the living room, remembering them all: passionate moments. Pancake moments. Wine-and-coffee-filled moments. Morning jogs. Laughter and fights. But there is pain. There is death. There are things here that don't erase the good times, and I really believe they will always shadow them gray.

Shaking off this idea, I walk to the kitchen and discover a huge basket filled with wine, chocolate, and fruit, a large yellow envelope next to it. The front door shuts and Shane appears in the doorway. "Do you know who would send this?"

"I'd bet it all on Freddy if I were in Vegas," he says, walking to the opposite side of the island to retrieve a small envelope that he hands to me.

I open it and remove the card to read aloud, *"Congratulations to the future Mr. and Mrs. Brandon. May you have a happy life together no matter where you might be, though I do believe it would be happier in New York. I hope the proposal I've included will make you believe that as well."* I look at Shane. "He's as determined as I am to get you to New York."

Shane opens the folder in his hand and pulls out a document, reading it for a full minute that has me ready to grab it and read it myself. "Well?"

He slides the document back into the envelope. "It means he got the nickname Maverick for a reason. He's offered Brandon Enterprises an opportunity to invest in a new division of the firm, with me running that division as a partner, therefore erasing my conflict of interest."

I try to tamp down the excitement he's stirring. "Does this mean you get your career back and we move to New York, away from Martina?"

"It means maybe. I need to do the due diligence with the firm and the board, but the board is really a non-issue. The bylaws give me a lot of latitude to act in the company's financial interest."

I lean on the island and study him. "But we both know the legal issues weren't the only issues holding you back, Shane."

"No. They were not. I need to read the contract and think on it." He walks around the counter and kisses me. "And then we'll talk. Okay?"

"Yes. Okay." He starts to walk away, and I fight the urge to catch his arm, but I let him go. He disappears into the other room and then into his office. I need to give him time to process in his own way.

I walk down the hallway to grab our bags but find they're already upstairs. I head that way and grab my journal from my bag, sitting on the bed with the intent of writing down everything I want to say to Shane. Instead I find myself sitting in a chair by the window and reading my first entry, two lines standing out to me:

See, I believe that when fear controls us, it makes decisions for us.

He feels guilt and blame, but that's where I have to shut it down for him as well. Because I choose Shane. And he chooses me.

I inhale and shut the journal with a realization. I used to write things down because I had no one I trusted with my feelings. I need to say these things to Shane, not write them down. I leave the journal on the bed and change my mind. I pick it up and take it with me, hurrying down the stairs, to the office. I find Shane behind his desk, but he's not reading the contract that is sitting on the wooden surface. He's leaning back in his chair, one booted foot on his knee, his fingers steepled in front of him.

I close the space between us and round the desk, placing myself between it and him. He straightens and lowers his leg. "I was going to write in this journal, but I'd rather talk to you."

His hands settle on my hips. "I want you to talk to me."

"But you aren't talking to me."

"That's not my intention."

"Well, then I'll start the conversation by asking you to read my journal entry." I open it and hand it to him. He studies me for several beats and then accepts the journal. I lean on the desk, bracing myself with my hands on the edge. His dark lashes lower and he begins to read. I watch him, looking for a reaction he doesn't offer. He just reads and then shuts the journal.

"Emily—"

"You saved the company," I say, before he can shut me down. "Derek is gone, and staying here doesn't save him. Giving up your job like I gave up Harvard doesn't help him. And you can't save your father. Your mother doesn't want to be saved. And as long as we're close to Martina, making him think about us, he's also thinking about everyone around us, and they don't have Cody."

He inhales, his eyes shutting, the lines of his face sharpening, seconds ticking by before he sets the journal on the desk and walks his chair closer to me, his hands coming down on my hips. "I do choose you, Emily, and I won't let fear, anger, or guilt make decisions for me. Let's go to New York."

"Really?"

"Yes. Really."

I breathe out, my hands settling on his shoulders. "I know there will be challenges, but . . ."

"We'll deal with the challenges later. Right now—"

I push off the desk and press my lips to his. He pulls me into his lap, his hand on the back of my head. "I take it this means you're happy?"

"Very happy."

"Show me," he says, turning my lips-pressed-to-lips kiss into a deep, drugging kiss, and at least for now, there are no challenges. There is no board to tell. There aren't his parents to manage. There is no Martina to surprise us. There's just me choosing him and him choosing me. For this moment that's all we want. The rest can wait.

CHAPTER TWENTY-TWO

Monday morning comes, and Shane and I arrive at work and ride the elevator to the lobby, him in a dark suit and red power tie, and me in a simple black skirt with a long-sleeved pale blue silk blouse, though there is nothing simple about the ring on my finger that I'm quite certain everyone will notice today. Starting with Jessica, who we are meeting with before heading upstairs.

We enter the coffee shop and find her already at a corner table, and the second she spots us, she stands up and points at the cups on the table.

"We need this woman in our lives," I say, a statement that has nothing to do with the coffee she's ordered for us and everything to do with her loyalty, skills, and friendship.

"She's going to come with us," he promises, aware of my worries, pulling a chair out of my path that was somehow left out of place.

"You can't know that," I say, noting how pretty she looks in a black dress, her newly extended blonde hair sleek and shiny. "What if there's a secret man in her life?"

He laughs. "You mean Cody?"

He's right. Those two flirt. Or she flirts and he tries not show his interest, but he does. And I really hate that his job makes her off-limits to him. My secret wish is that he breaks protocol and just grabs her and kisses her really well, and soon.

We join her at the table and she settles her hands on top. "So. What are we talking about that required a semi-secret rendezvous? Or as close to one as I'll ever get?"

"We have big plans," I say. "And we want you to be a big part of those big plans."

"You have my attention," she says. "Are designer clothes with the Brandon name on them involved?"

"How about a Jessica line?"

Her eyes go wide. "What? A Jessica line? I don't understand."

"Like there is Ralph Lauren Polo Sport and—"

"And you want there to be a Jessica line for Brandon Style?"

"With stock and profit incentives," Shane adds.

She leans forward and stares at Shane, then taps two fingers on the table in front of him. "If I were to jump up and down and shout before hugging you and then Emily right here and now, you would not be pleased, correct?"

"No," Shane agrees. "I would not be pleased."

"That sucks," she says. "Because I really want to jump up and down and—"

"The job will be in New York," Shane says. "Emily and I are moving there, and we're planning to relocate a portion of the company there as well."

"I'll need a cost of living raise to go with the incentives," she says immediately.

"Done," Shane says.

I laugh. "Well, that was very efficient and businesslike," I say. "We'll shout and jump for joy in his office later." I reach for my coffee, and her eyes land on my ring.

"Oh my God." She grabs my hand. "Is this——" She looks at Shane. "You did this without my help and you did it well." She doesn't give him time to reply. "You should leave before I start screaming now. You also have a conference call in"——she glances at her watch——"ten minutes."

"Well, then," Shane says. "Let the screaming begin." He kisses me. "Come see me when you're done." He stands and leaves.

"To think I once threatened to hurt you if you hurt him," she says. "Actually, that still stands." She sobers. "He's a good man in a bad family. I wanted him and me to be a thing once. Did I tell you that?" She doesn't wait for a reply. "We just have zero chemistry. But you two. You were magic the moment I saw you together." She sighs. "I almost believe in fairy tales again, but then I look at his family."

I sip my coffee, feeling that dizzy, queasy feeling again.

"Why did you just turn green?" Jessica asks.

"I don't know. I'm feeling strange."

She leans forward. "Are you pregnant?"

"No. Of course not. I take precautions. I was in Manhattan with all those people. I probably just caught a bug." My stomach starts to churn. "I think I need to get to my office."

"Of course, sweetie," she says, and we head for the door, then the elevator. "Have you talked about a date?" she asks once we're inside.

I lean against the wall, feeling as green as she says I am. "Not yet."

"Have you told his parents?"

"Not yet."

"Have you thought about a dress?"

"Dress?"

"Yes. A dress. Guest list. And a location—"

Now I'm really sick, I think, tuning her out. Guests? I have no guests to invite. I have no family. The elevator dings and she says, "Have you considered having our new designer design you a Brandon Style original for your dress?"

For the wedding with a guest list and lots of people I don't know. "I need to step into the ladies' room," I say, but as I exit the elevator, I come face-to-face with Shane's mother.

"Oh, thank goodness," Maggie says. "David wants tea. Can you get him that tea you know he likes? His throat hurts, probably from yelling at his new assistant."

"Of course," Jessica says, taking my coffee and handing it to her. "We were just bringing him a tea. And now we have a meeting."

I take my coffee from Maggie. "They got the order wrong. He'll be upset if you give him that."

Maggie's lips curve, and she takes the coffee from me and then turns and walks back to the office.

"What just happened?" Jessica asks.

"I'm going to contemplate that while staring at a porcelain bowl." I start forward and into the bathroom, but as soon as I open the stall door, I'm no longer sick.

I turn around and walk to the sink as Jessica enters. "That's the wrong porcelain bowl," she says. "It doesn't flush."

"I'm oddly okay now," I say, sitting down in the chair against the wall.

"Are you sure you can't be pregnant?"

"I'm not," I say. "And it would be bad if I were."

"Why? You'd be amazing parents."

"It's a bad time, Jessica. Let us get married before you start planning our family."

"Right. The wedding—"

"I have no one to invite." I push to my feet.

"Emily——"

"I need to get to work." I step around her and head for the door, making my way to my office, where I walk to my desk and sit down. My lashes lower, and I think of the wedding, but then I think of the possibility of being pregnant. I can't be. But did they give me my meds in the hospital? I haven't missed a period. This is ridiculous.

My intercom buzzes. "I need you, Ms. Stevens," Brandon Senior says while Shane appears in my doorway, irritation sliding across his features at his father's command. He holds up a finger and points, indicating he's going to talk to him, and I hold up my hand and shake my head.

"Ms. Stevens," Brandon senior says again. "I said I need you."

"What you need," I say, "is to be kinder to your assistants, of which I am not any longer. And your wife. And your son. Your tea order is on file at the register downstairs. And I have work to do other than fetch it for you."

The line is quiet, and then his soft laughter fills the room. "You are a piece of work, Ms. Stevens." He ends the connection.

Shane laughs and shuts the door, crossing to my side of the desk. I turn my chair to face him, and he leans in and rests his hands on either side of me. "I have no one to invite to the wedding either."

"Jessica told you. I should have told her not to."

"You should have talked to me."

"I would have. You know I would have. That's why she should have just let me talk to you. I didn't even think about the guest list until she brought it up. And I don't want to let this affect your ideal wedding."

"My ideal wedding is the one where you say 'I do.' Men

don't dream of fancy weddings, sweetheart. We dream of our perfect woman, and you're mine."

My heart squeezes. "Shane," I whisper. "I—"

The intercom buzzes. "Sorry, you two," Jessica says. "But Seth says he needs to speak to you both urgently."

My heart thunders with fear for my brother. "Send him in," I say.

"Relax, sweetheart," Shane says. "I'm sure Rick is fine." He pushes off the chair and faces forward as Seth enters the room. And if Denver is danger, Seth in a suit, looking stone-faced and like he might kill someone at any moment, is most definitely at least a big dose of trouble.

"There's nothing wrong," he says, shutting the door behind him. "I just need to run something by you both."

"Urgently?" I ask suspiciously. "And nothing is wrong?"

"When conversation comes before action," Seth says, stepping between the two visitor chairs in front of my desk, "I consider conversation urgent. I'll get to the point." He looks at me. "Finding your brother wasn't easy. He's skilled. He's smart. He chose Germany to disappear in because there's an underground hacker society there that makes disappearing easy to do."

Shane bristles beside me. "Did we lose him?"

"No," Seth says. "As I said, we have a female hacker with him and she's on our payroll. But that could change, and quickly. I can tell you from my years in the CIA that hackers are necessary evils. We pay them. Someone pays them more. Then they're gone. Relying on hired help in another country indefinitely is not a realistic long-term plan."

"A problem we obviously knew about when we took this route with Rick," Shane points out.

"I knew when Nick set this up that I needed a solution that worked beyond this temporary fix, but I couldn't act on a maybe.

We had to have him in our sights first, which is why I went to the CIA and began a negotiation the minute we found him."

"The CIA?" I ask. "What negotiation would you do for my brother with the CIA?"

"I informed them that I have a hacking asset connected to the Geminis, which I knew would get their attention. Bottom line here: if we, if I, hand over Rick to them, he becomes their asset, not mine, and they'll keep him alive and out of jail."

I inhale and let the breath out, trying to process the implications of this strange development. "So if you hand him over to them, he's a prisoner or an agent?"

"Both, if you stretch the interpretations of those words," Seth says, a perplexing answer.

I try the question another way. "How do we ensure he stays with the CIA once he's with the CIA?"

"The division that would be managing Rick is well-equipped to manage lifelong assets."

It's yet another non-answer, but before I can push for more, Shane interjects, shutting down the idea altogether with, "This connects Emily to Rick. They will look at his history. He set up her Emily Stevens identification. If the CIA then looks for her, a leak to the Geminis about her could follow." His voice firms. "I don't like it. This doesn't work."

"Emily is dead to everyone, including the government. It does work. But if you want additional peace of mind, you've got it." He eyes my hand on the counter, where the ring glistens, before his attention returns to Shane. "A last name change further dilutes her identity. But I'd do that sooner rather than later."

Shane studies him several beats. "We'll also be relocating to New York," he says, the question seeming to suggest that he's feeling better about this plan.

"Another smart move," Seth confirms. "And distance from

Martina is for the best. The more he sees and thinks about you, the more likely he thinks up another business proposition using you as a tool."

"I'll be taking a partner role in my old firm," Shane explains, "while Brandon Enterprises takes a financial role. I'd like you to consider relocating as well."

"You know I prefer New York." He glances between us. "Are we moving forward with my plan?"

I glance at Shane. "Yes."

He looks at Seth. "Yes. How soon will it be done?"

"Twenty-four hours."

"Do it," Shane says.

Seth's response is his standard nod and exit. The minute the door shuts, Shane turns me to him and pulls me to my feet. The next moment I'm between him and the desk. "You're good with this?"

"Yes. It feels like well-timed finality."

"He said get married quickly. Let's elope."

"What? But don't you—"

"Want to marry you as soon as possible? Yes. I do."

"I . . . Elope where?"

"Wherever you want, but let's get away for a week. There are laws and waiting times in other countries, but we can get married here and then fly out. Rome. Italy. Ireland."

"Ireland," I say. "I'd love to go to Ireland."

"Ireland it is then. I'll work on the arrangements, but let's make it fast. Next weekend."

"What about the firm in New York?"

"They'll survive a week's wait and so will anything here." He cups my face. "I love you, Emily." He kisses me. "Let's go home and work. We'll fly back to New York and plan next weekend from there."

"I have interviews this afternoon."

"Have them meet you at the hotel restaurant." He releases me. "Grab your purse. What else do you need?"

"Nothing."

"Good." His jaw sets and he adds, "We have one last thing to do on the way out the door." He takes my hand in his and leads me down the hall, and he doesn't stop at the lobby. We pass the receptionist and enter the private lobby for his father, walking right past the new secretary. Shane opens his father's door and we enter, shutting it behind us.

Maggie gasps as she pops out of his father's lap. "Son!"

"A knock, Son," Brandon Senior bites out, "would be respectful."

"Emily and I are eloping," Shane announces.

Brandon Senior arches a brow but says nothing.

"We're also relocating to New York."

"New York!" Maggie gasps. "What about the business?"

"It will be just fine," Shane assures them, and I don't miss that they haven't asked about the elopement. Shane turns, opens the door, and we exit without Brandon Senior saying a word. Not one. And we don't stop walking until we step onto an elevator car. And the instant the doors seal us inside, he pulls me to him, his forehead to mine. "It's just you and me, sweetheart. It has been since the day we met."

He's right. It has been. And I realize now, more than ever, just how alone we are. How alone we both were before a cup of coffee, and some lipstick, ended up on the wrong lips and changed everything.

CHAPTER TWENTY-THREE

We learn that my brother is in CIA custody before we leave two days later for New York, and I am both relieved and nervous, but not for myself. For Rick. As his sister, I can't help but want him to have a new beginning of his own.

Our new beginning is officially underway. Shane moves forward with the partnership, and the board is actually excited about the opportunity it represents. And Shane is ready to make it happen. Once he made the decision to rejoin the firm, he became fire unleashed, both in and out of the bedroom, and I can't wait to see what he will do in the future. He's so ready for this change that we pack up what we can in Denver for a mover and leave only the necessities for random trips. We do make one agreement I didn't count on: Cody will be with us for three months, outside of our honeymoon. Just to be safe. I readily agree, deciding that if this allows Shane to focus and get past the loss of his brother, then so be it.

By the weekend, Shane and I have picked out his wedding band, also at Tiffany's. Jessica, Seth, and now Cody are also in

New York with us, making company and personal decisions to coordinate their moves and the company's, and Seth has just delivered my passport. We've also received a pizza delivery and retreated to our "thinking room" to talk about where to get married. "Here," I say. "I like this room."

"It's too small for Seth and Jessica to be witnesses," he says. "And it's our room. Just ours."

Which is what I like about it, I think. It's ours. We won't feel like anyone else who isn't there should be there. Like his parents, who haven't even called to ask about the wedding. "Somewhere else in the apartment?" I ask. "Or the patio?"

"It's New York in the summer and hot."

"Hmmm," I say.

He sighs and picks up a slice of pizza but sets it back down. "I know this is unorthodox, but what if we do it inside the private plane we charter to Ireland? It easily fits the preacher, a photographer to give us some memory shots, and Seth, Cody, and Jessica."

I consider the idea, and it feels right. Like a place that isn't what everyone else expects. Like a place that is ours, and the few people who are with us are helping see us off to a new adventure for not just a week but a lifetime. "Yes. Yes. Let's do it."

"Perfect," he says, kissing me. "I'll take care of everything."

The next morning I wake up feeling sick again, and I decide it's nerves. I'm getting married. And I have no dress. Shane heads to a meeting with Freddy, and since I don't have to go anywhere today, I'm in sweats with no makeup on, sitting on the bed and surfing the web for a wedding dress. And I fail miserably at finding one. I call Jessica. "I need a dress. I don't know what to wear."

The doorbell rings. "Answer your door and you will."

My brow furrows. "What does that mean?"

"Shane loves you. Answer the door."

I have no clue what she is talking about, but I hurry down the hallway and to the door, pulling it open to find Jessica and our new designer, Luc, a tall, thin, regal-looking man in a suit. "I hear you need a dress," he says, looking me and my sweats up and down. "And possibly more."

"You're going to make me a dress? Can you do that this fast?"

"No," he says. "I cannot. Which is why I called all my famous designer friends." He motions me in the door, and suddenly racks of dresses are being rolled into the apartment by several people who work for him.

My cell phone rings, and I pull it from my phone to see Shane's number. "I can't believe you did this."

"I told you I'd take care of everything, sweetheart. Enjoy yourself. I'll see you soon."

And I am pretty sure my face is going to break, I'm smiling so big.

Hours later I've battled queasiness throughout the entire dress selection process, and Jessica has her judgmental eye on me. Thankfully, since I haven't been feeling well, my three pounds of pancake butt have disappeared, or I'm fairly certain Luc would have had a cardiac arrest, as I soon discover he does with anything that fits too big or too small. Despite all of this, I have fun trying on dresses, some crazy, some sexy, some quirky, and I find the perfect gown.

It's knee length and pink lace, not white, with sheer sleeves and a deep-V neckline that has a sheer shell to match the sleeves. I slip on a pair of pink heels Luc just happens to have on the show rack, and model my pick. Luc, his three staff members, and Jessica all clap.

"Champagne time!" Luc shouts, and somehow he is pro-
ducing a bottle and filling glasses.

But when mine is handed to me, Jessica takes it and downs
it. "Take a test first or at least wait until you start your period.
When is it due?"

"Would you believe on my wedding day?" I ask.

"Oh, Mother Nature is a bitch, isn't she? Why not take a
test?"

"I don't think I am, but if I am . . . I don't know."

Her hands come down on my shoulders. "He'll be happy.
Take the test."

"Can you get me one? I don't want Cody to know."

She walks to her purse and returns with a bag. "I picked it
up on the way over."

"Thank you."

"Call me."

"I will."

She and Luc's team leave, and I rush to the bathroom and
take the test. It's negative. I take another one. It's negative too.
I'm relieved. I'm sad. I think I'm sad. No, I'm not. I want this
kind of decision to be ours together.

The night before the wedding, Shane stays with Seth, who I
discover has an apartment a few blocks away that he's owned
for years. He suggests I invite Jessica over, but I just really
want to be alone and process where I've come from and where
I'm going. I also want to enjoy our bathtub without sharing.
Shane calls me before bed, and we talk for an hour before he
ends the call with a soft, sexy, "Tomorrow, sweetheart."

"Tomorrow," I whisper, and I'm smiling again, but this
time, I imagine I look rather whimsical.

Morning arrives and I'm nervous, my stomach all crazy

again. And I haven't started my period. "Stress can do this," Jessica says when I call her. "But I'll pick up another test."

"Thank you."

An hour later my hair and makeup are done, and Cody drives me to the airport, where my dress and Jessica await. Nerves dance in my belly, and I decide nerves really could be the issue with the nausea. I step on the plane and gasp as I find it filled with dozens of pink roses. There is an attendant standing in front of me, a smile on her lips as she hands me a card. I open it and it reads: *Because they remind me of you. Shane.*

The flight attendant moves aside, and I'm pleased to discover the plane has limited seating and plenty of standing room. Jessica appears in the walkway, wearing a white slip dress, as we've planned, that is simple but elegant. "And he didn't even know what color your dress was," she says, lifting her hand to the roses. "I didn't tell him." She motions me forward. "Ready to put it on?"

"Yes," I say, hurrying toward her. "And the test?"

"I left it in the car," she says. "My hands were full. I'll grab it in a few, but maybe you shouldn't take it before the wedding. You can't change the outcome now, and if it's positive, it will affect you."

"You're right. I want to just think about him right now. And you know. I can't be pregnant. I drank wine. I got tipsy. That would be bad."

She steps in front of me and settles her hands on my arms. "People drink a glass of wine here and there while pregnant now. They allow it."

"But I got tipsy."

"You are fine. You aren't going to get sloppy drunk all the time. You aren't going to drink at all, I can tell."

"I'm not pregnant."

"Think about the wedding."

"Yes. I love Shane."

"And he loves you, so think about Shane." She glances at her watch. "The photographer will be here any minute." She releases me. "Go now. Hurry and dress."

I move to a curtain she's set up and quickly change into cream-colored thigh-highs and a lacy bra and panty set I bought for today. My strappy pink heels are next and then the dress. My final touch is my mother's bracelet. *If only she could be here now.* I've barely stepped out from behind the curtain before Jessica frets over my hair and makeup before declaring me "beautiful."

And just in time, as the photographer arrives, and for thirty minutes he's turning me left and right, snapping shots. Finally he's done, and Cody steps onto the plane in a tuxedo. Jessica grabs my arm. "Hello, Latin lover," she murmurs softly, which draws a much-needed laugh.

"The preacher is here," he says. "Shane's talking to him, and then we'll have the three of them join us."

"Okay." I breathe out, soft music beginning to play, but I don't hear the words. Seth steps onto the plane in a tuxedo, followed by the man I assume to be the preacher. I assume right, because he rushes to me and shakes my hand, but I barely hear him. I'm nervous and excited and Shane . . . I just want Shane.

Jessica directs everyone to their positions, and the attendant who'd given me the note walks up to me and hands me a gorgeous bouquet of pink roses. "Thank you," I whisper, and when she steps aside, Shane is standing there, looking incredible in a tuxedo—the epitome of tall, dark, and handsome. And the warmth in his eyes is overwhelming. My heart swells, and when he steps to my side and takes my hand, I have never felt the love I feel for him for anyone. I have never felt as loved as I feel in this moment. The ceremony is short, simple, our vows of love and forever spoken for us and no one else. The kiss he gives me is passionate, intense.

And when it's over, it's a beginning, not an end. We share hugs with everyone, and right before Jessica leaves, she hands me a gift bag. She then hugs me and whispers, "Whatever the result, it's the right result."

She leaves and the doors shut. I walk to Shane and he grabs the bottle sticking out of the top of the ice bucket. "Sparkling cider?"

My eyes go wide and I swallow hard. "I've been sick."

"I thought that passed?"

"It didn't."

"Are you saying   "

"I don't know. I took a test last week and it was negative and I've been taking my birth control, but I started thinking about the hospital and right when I got home. And, Shane, I didn't start my period today." I pull the box from the bag. "Jessica brought me another test. I don't think I can be, but—"

"Take another test," he says. "Go take it."

"Yes. Okay."

I walk to the bathroom and he follows me, standing outside the door as I go inside. I tear open the box and I'm shaking a little inside and out.

"Did you take it?" he asks.

"Just now. It's . . ." My eyes go wide and he opens the door.

"It's what?"

I turn to face him. "It's—I'm—"

"We're pregnant," he supplies, clearly able to form the words that I cannot.

"Yes," I whisper. "Are you—"

He pulls me to him and kisses me. "Happy? Yes. I am. I

didn't expect to be, but I am. Because you, Emily Brandon, are *my wife* and soon to be the mother of my child. Because, somehow, you manage to give me everything I don't know I want and prove it's everything I do want and even need."

And I think I might cry if I could stop smiling and if he wasn't kissing me again.

Dear Readers,

Typing "the end" is as surreal for me as Reagan's death was for Emily! It was torture to write Derek's death, and even though I'd known all along he would die, I almost changed my mind! But there were so many ways Derek's death changed Shane and defined his future. There are many ways his death could affect the events that happen in the future. If Emily's brother ever shows back up, can you imagine how Derek's actions will affect how Shane reacts to that threat?

But as I sit here imagining what could come next, there is nothing planned as of yet. But! I'd love to write more about Emily and Shane. Already I'm imagining her freak out as she remembers the wine she drank before knowing she was pregnant. I'm thinking of her working from home to be with the baby and opening her offices in the same building as the mall, right next door to Shane's law firm. And when all is well, Martina returns! Or Emily's brother.

Or not.

I do not know if I will write more of Shane and Emily at this point, but I will be writing Seth's story. There is a woman in Seth's past who will soon be in his future too. I'm very excited to share how he became the cold, calculating "fixer." Look for this in 2018. And Jessica. Oh, how I love Jessica. I think she needs her Latin love in Cody, and soon! I must write Jessica's story. I hope you think so as well.

With all this said, I am not quite ready to be done with this chapter of the story. For that reason, I want to leave you with a scene from *Bad Deeds* that was never published, as a thank-you for taking this Dirty Money journey with me. Just as a little context, this takes place after Adrian's uninvited visit to Shane and Emily's apartment in *Bad Deeds*, when Adrian makes a business proposition to Shane that includes full infiltration of his drug cartel in Brandon Pharmaceuticals. Of course, neither Shane nor Emily reacts well to this, and you saw the initial scene from Shane's POV, but I originally wrote it in Emily's, which is what you'll read below! I hope you enjoy it!

Xoxo,
Lisa

ALTERNATE SCENE FROM *BAD DEEDS*

EMILY

Shane closes the small space between us, and the force of dark torment I'd seen, felt, and even tasted on his lips in the elevator earlier pales to the dominance and power he radiates now. I can almost feel the iron control he's erected around himself, and I wonder if this is the aftermath of standing toe-to-toe with the drug lord he's just agreed to do business with, a fact that I can barely get my head around. Something happened out there on that patio between Shane and Adrian Martina that I don't quite understand. It wasn't friendship, but it wasn't the absolute divide I'd expected either.

Shane stops in front of me but doesn't touch me, as if he's weighing my mood, my reaction to his nearness and the meeting I just witnessed, and therefore I dictate his next move. "Everything you heard out there was about strategy," he says.

"Strategy?" I demand tightly, disliking the way he's repeated Adrian Martina's words. "Are you really telling me that you're willingly going to go into business with that man?"

"We're already in business with him," he says. "I'm trying to limit our exposure while I get him the hell out of my company, and do so without getting us all killed."

"In other words, you're going into business with him."

"I told you—"

"You're already in business with him," I repeat, and desperate to force another answer, another solution, I reach for a way out. "Martina doesn't want to do business with Derek. He knows he's a risk."

"I think he made that quite clear tonight," he says before I can go on.

"Right. Exactly. He wants you, and if you aren't involved, maybe he walks away. So you walk away first, now. Give the company to your brother and let's go to New York and you—"

"Derek will end up dead and you know I won't let that happen."

He's right, so I try another approach. "Go to the FBI. Negotiate a way to save your family."

"The FBI's a two-headed beast. The good agents will turn us into snitches, which equates to dead or in hiding. The bad ones will run straight to Martina. So no. I cannot go to the FBI."

I believe him, and while the corruption and limits upon us should be what bother me, they are not. At least not in this moment. It's the interaction between him and Martina niggling at me, insisting I revisit it. "What was that I witnessed between you and Martina? There was—"

"Strategy," he repeats, and his hands go to my waist, firm, warm, possessive. "You witnessed strategy."

"Strategy? Playing nice with a drug lord is strategy?"

And in a blink he's maneuvered us both, and I'm now pressed against the couch, his powerful legs framing mine. "I need you to trust me to handle this."

"This isn't about trusting you, Shane. It's about protecting you. It's about helping you."

"I protect you," he says. "You don't protect me."

I blanch. "What? No. We protect each other. That's how it is or we aren't who I think we are."

"Right now, in this, it is. It's me protecting you. I need you to let me do what I need to do."

"What you *need* to do? What do you need to do, Shane?"

His jaw clenches. "Let me handle this, Emily."

"So that's it?" I demand, feeling that door I'd sworn wasn't shut back in the elevator shut now. "You handle this? I stand on the outside and pray you come out alive?" My jaw sets. "No," I repeat. "I won't do that. I can't do that."

"You will. The end."

It's a sharp command that induces shock, which is quickly followed by anger I fight to rein in. He's been through hell today. He's not himself. He doesn't need a war with me on top of everything else. "Let me off the couch, Shane," I say softly, pressing on his chest. "Let me go."

"I'm not letting you go, Emily."

It's clear to me that he's not talking about this moment, but I am. "Let me go before I forget that all the hell you went through tonight is the source of your assholeness. Because I'm really trying, but—"

He tangles his fingers in my hair, tilting my face to his, adrenaline rushing through my veins. "This isn't about me being an asshole, Emily," he declares, his voice low, gravelly. "Distancing you from all of this, anyway I can, is about protecting you. What part of that do you not understand?"

"What part of 'I have to protect you' do *you* not understand?" I counter, gripping his arms. "I have to protect you. Don't you see that, Shane? *I need*—"

His mouth slants over mine, swallowing my words, his tongue licking into my mouth in a long, deep stroke followed by another, and I can taste his emotions in his kiss again. The anger. The torment. The *lust*. Oh yes. There is lust. There is hunger. So much hunger. It expands in every passing moment, rising up, demanding notice, until it has a living, breathing life of its own. Until I'm not sure if it's his or mine. It consumes me, a drug on my tongue that sizzles through my blood and controls me. It controls him too. I can feel it in the way he steps into me, deepening the kiss, his kiss, the long, hard lines of his body somehow harder now, and I want all those sinewy muscles next to mine.

I sway into him, trying to get closer, but abruptly he tears his mouth from mine and his body lifts, breaking our connection. "Shane," I pant out, his name a plea and a question I don't even intend to ask but that I want answered.

His fingers tighten ever so slightly, erotically, in my hair, his lips lingering a breath from another touch, and I can almost taste his lust, his need, but still he holds back. Seconds tick by, the air thickening with my blood until I can no longer breathe. "Shane," I whisper, gripping his shirt, holding on tighter, and I think that's what he needs, even if he doesn't know it. For me to hold on tighter. Or maybe that's what I need.

He reaches down and covers my hand as if he's telling me yes. Hold on. He'll hold on too, and I silently vow then, that yes. We will. His family, my family, will not tear us apart. *"I need,"* he breathes out, his breath tickling my lips again. "And every sentence I start with those words right now," he adds, his voice low, gravelly, "ends with you naked and me inside you."

Heat rushes though me with the words that promise the satisfaction of every fantasy he's stirred in me tonight. "Then why do we still have clothes on?"

"This is just fucking. No talking," he says, his teeth nipping my lobe, his fingers tugging free the knot I've made at the bottom of my blouse. "Just fucking," he adds, licking the pinch left from his teeth and sending a shiver down my spine before he yanks free the remaining buttons on my shirt. His head lifting, his gaze meeting mine, the lust I'd tasted on his lips now burning in the blue flecks of his grayer-than-gray eyes. And the dark hunger I'd tasted on his lips and mine is now etched in every handsome line of his chiseled face. "Just fucking," he repeats, reaching down to unsnap and then unzip my pants before cupping my face. "No making love right now, Emily. That's not what this is. That's not what tonight is. Do you understand? I need—"

"I know what you need," I say, feeling the rage of his emotions as my own. Maybe it is my own. Maybe he's unleashed what I've buried. Like coming home to everything I've run from and battled for months on end, and with it the understanding of what he wants: escape. Moments in time when that monster in his mind and heart taunts him with every betrayal and heartache he is living, when he can't find a voice or a blade.

His hands go back to the couch, arms catching me, his stare probing, while my body is warm all over, the low throb of craving touching me everywhere he is not. And he's not touching me. He's just studying me, searching for something that I don't know he's looking for, perhaps searching for how much he dare show me. How much he dare demand. Yes. That is what he wants to know and I answer the question he hasn't asked. "I know what you need," I repeat, hunger beginning to claw at me, like my fears over Shane and Martina's relationship, which is more than it should be, easier than I expected it to be.

Still, though, Shane doesn't move, and while I have nothing

but a feeling to go on, I sense him fighting for control over the beast that is his emotions, as if unleashing it is unleashing those feelings, commanding them. But I don't want him to command these things. Not now. I know what it's like to bottle those emotions, to force them into submission and struggle at random moments when they try to surface. Letting them go on his terms is control, and I reach forward and begin unknotting his tie.

His eyes sharpen and he releases me to take over, pulling the blue silk from his collar. "Lace your fingers together in front of you."

I suck in air with the realization that he means to tie me up, to perhaps control me, when he can control nothing else. My old demons raise their angry heads with this knowledge, those demons that let me be controlled and manipulated in an almost self-punishing fashion. And when I search Shane's face and look into his eyes, and as I look into his eyes, I see a question. Will I trust him? Do I trust him? And it's then I realize that perhaps he needs me to trust him now, to trust himself? I think. . . . yes. Yes, that is what he's asking and what he needs. He needs me to be the one person in his life who trusts him unconditionally. And I discover something about myself with this assessment. After all the letdowns and betrayal in my life, I need to both give and receive unconditional trust as well.

Decision made, holding his stare, I bring my palms together in between us and fold my fingers. His eyes narrow, his gaze locked with mine, his expression unreadable. He doesn't move, seconds ticking by with no action, no movement, no touch. "Shane," I whisper, his name a plea, seeking a reaction or really *an action*, which he gives me. I blink, and before I know what's happening, I'm facing the couch and he's already skimming the silk of my blouse down my arms, cool air washing over my warm skin. In another moment, my bra is unhooked, the straps falling forward and down my arms. It drops to the ground and Shane kicks it away, his big, hard body arching around mine, his hands pressing my hands against the couch, the thick ridge of his erection nuzzling my backside.

His cheek settles next to mine, and I inhale his spicy, masculine scent, sensations rolling through me, and I swear I can almost taste the raw hunger radiating off him. He wants and just as he said: he needs. And just as those things are palpable, so is his battle to fight those things and how they affect him. As if he's mentally talking himself down, telling himself to shelter me, to protect me from something inside him he fears I can't handle. Maybe he doesn't even know that part of himself, but I want to know him, all of him. Maybe he doesn't want me to know that part of him, and this hits a nerve.

"If you don't trust me," I say, remembering every man in my life, from my father to my brother and in between who showed me only pieces of who and what they were, "then why am I here?"

He turns me around to face him, the couch at my back, his powerful thighs framing mine, his hands at my waist, his brow furrowed. "You think I don't trust you?"

"You asked for my trust and I gave it to you. I know you're holding back. I know you don't want to share—"

"I don't want to scare you away."

My hand flattens on his chest. "You can't scare me away, Shane."

HEADLINE
ETERNAL

FIND YOUR HEART'S DESIRE...

VISIT OUR WEBSITE: www.headlineeternal.com
FIND US ON FACEBOOK: facebook.com/eternalromance
CONNECT WITH US ON TWITTER: @eternal_books
FOLLOW US ON INSTAGRAM: @headlineeternal
EMAIL US: eternalromance@headline.co.uk